Career
Success
with
Pets

HOW TO
GET STARTED, GET GOING,
GET AHEAD

Career Success with Pets

HOW TO
GET STARTED, GET GOING,
GET AHEAD

Kim Barber

HOWELL
BOOK
HOUSE

MACMILLAN • USA

Howell Book House
MACMILLAN
A Simon & Schuster/Macmillan Company
1633 Broadway
New York, NY 10019

MACMILLAN is a registered trademark of Macmillan, Inc.

Library of Congress Cataloging-in-Publication Data
Barber, Kim.
    Career success with pets : how to get started, get going, get ahead / Kim Barber.
            P.   cm.
        ISBN 0-87605-768-7
    1. Pet industry. 2. Pet industry—Vocational guidance. 3. Small business.
    4. New business enterprises. I. Title.
    SF414.7.B37   1996
    636.088'7'068—dc20   95-38134
                                                                CIP

Manufactured in the United States of America
10 9 8 7 6 5 4 3 2 1

TABLE OF CONTENTS

INTRODUCTION

···

THERE IS NOTHING GREATER THAN
BEING YOUR OWN BOSS!

However, nothing holds more responsibilities than owning and operating your own business. If you believe that you can run a small business successfully, and enjoy the idea of being self-employed while working with pets and the public, then you probably have what it takes for career success with pets.

Thoroughly research any field before entering it. Never embark on any investment, alteration in lifestyle or career change without professional advice, legal counsel, or assistance.

First, I would suggest that you enroll in a small-business course at your local college where you will acquire information invaluable to operating a small business. This information will include bookkeeping, market research, accounting, estimating your profits, business analysis and other general information specifically geared to small-business ownership or management.

Pets are our partners. They share this earth with us and are entitled to love, care and respect. Each animal has a particular behavior and temperament. By recognizing and accepting each animal's individual character, we gain a deeper understanding and greater appreciation of that ani mal, as well as a greater sense of personal accomplishment.

Kennel Management

Commercial Boarding Kennels—Dogs and Cats

KENNEL OWNER OR OPERATOR

A boarding kennel is a facility that houses animals in the owner's absence. It may be a simple operation, with just a few indoor or outdoor runs, or it may be an elaborate "motel" with private air conditioned/heated suites, music, sauna room, and gourmet meals.

Whatever type of boarding establishment you plan to operate, you should be aware of the sizable commitment involved in running it. The positive points include working from home (usually), being your own boss, working with animals and earning a comfortable income. However, the drawbacks are plentiful; for example, you will never be able to take a vacation, you will work seven days a week, you cannot take off for holidays, you will be expected to maintain a strict ethical code, you will spend most of your time cleaning and occasionally you will have to handle vicious, scared or ill animals.

Checking the Legalities

Several states have laws governing boarding kennels. You should check with the health department of the state in which you plan to operate your kennel. Also, you should contact your county's building department concerning construction codes, noise ordinances and zoning laws. You might need a sales license if you plan on marketing merchandise, or feed, in your reception area. Additionally, your city might require a license to operate a retail establishment and it is advisable to contact them regarding this.

Kennel Design

Your kennel will consist of the building *and* the grounds. When designing your kennel you must include heating, air conditioning, and cross ventilation. Although difficult, it is absolutely necessary to reduce the moisture level and keep humidity down in a kennel. Airborne disease organisms need moisture to remain alive. Simply reducing the humidity level from 90 to 80 percent can reduce dangerous airborne microbe numbers by half!

The following list will help you in your construction design:

Enclosures   Your kennel enclosures should consist of inside and outside runs. Other enclosures will be indoor wall banks (usually needed to house small animals), isolation banks, and exercise runs. The exercise runs should be long enough to allow the animals ample but safe space for running.

Kitchen/Utility   This area will be where you prepare the food and launder the bedding. You will need: a food cart, refrigerator, freezer, stove, washer and dryer, sink, shelves and a separate storage room.

Bathroom   This is a requirement (by law) if you intend to have employees.

Kennel owners must make sure clients' pets remain as happy and healthy as when they arrived.

Isolation Room   This room will be used for the isolation of animals suspected of harboring an illness. It should be used if *any indication* of illness appears, as you must protect the health of the other animals in your boarding facility. The isolation room should have an adequate ventilation system. All employees should be required to wear gloves, or thoroughly cleanse their hands, after handling any animal in the isolation room. Additionally, a vet should be notified immediately upon any signs of illness in your kennel.

Grooming Area   The grooming area is a separate area used only for grooming the animals. You will need a tub, grooming tables, dryers, and grooming tools.

Training Area   This is optional. If you would like to include a training area in your design you must allow for space. A training area should be allowed the maximum amount of grounds space possible.

Storage Room   Used for storing feed. The storage room should be kept locked at all times.

Office or Reception Area   This will be the area where your customers will check their dogs "in" and "out." It should be attractive and inviting. Some popular colors for this room are combinations of peach and aqua blue; magenta and teal blue; blue and green, a combination that radiates a tranquil and peaceful atmosphere; and the newest "hot" colors, orange and hot pink. Additionally, you should use this area for sales, if you decide to sell pet products or pet food as an addition to your boarding business. Successful marketing of premium pet foods can actually translate into a higher profit for your boarding operation, in some cases, than the profit produced by boarding itself.

You may wish to start small and add on at a later date. Most kennels have the capacity to hold 50–100 animals. However, some kennels have only a 5–10 dog or cat capacity. When building, try to estimate whether you'll need a larger or smaller kennel by figuring in your location and your kennel's competition. You could design your kennel building to house a larger number of pets, yet only install half the number of runs. Then, if your business is successful and you wish to expand, you can easily add the remaining half of the runs to your building.

KENNELING CATS

Cat Room　The cats you board should be kept in an area separated from the dogs to prevent any undue stress on the cats.

Cattery Caging　It should have large indoor/outdoor runs that reach from floor to ceiling. Cages with carpeted scratching posts and soft, warm beds both lessen stress and raise the comfort quotient. There should be shelving for cat perches, trees for climbing, toys, covered litter trays, and enough space to place the water and feed dishes a minimum of 36 inches away from the litter tray. I do not advocate or encourage the use of small cages. I have seen cats spend their entire lives in a cage with room enough only for a litter tray and a bowl of water. Never, never, *never* house an animal under these conditions.

Feeding   Feed your cats out of heavy (to prevent tipping) glass bowls, as some cats will get a rash on the chin from plastic. Others will not eat from plastic because the odor of old food tends to remain in this material.

Cattery Building   It should have heating, air conditioning, exhaust fans, and an air cleaning system. Smoke and fire alarms are a must! Piped-in music is a nice touch, and having two cats per "suite," when appropriate, will provide your cats with companionship.

Lighting   should be considered important in any cattery. If your cats are to be kept strictly indoors, try to give them access to natural light through large, uncovered windows or sun roofs. If natural light is not available, fluorescent lamps are advised. There are manufacturers who produce artificial daylight fluorescent tubes. Although they cost a bit more, they're well worth it.

Air Flow   Another important factor in your cattery should be air flow. Exhaust fans, air exchangers, or window fans should be used to approximate an average change of air as much as four to six times per hour. Air exchange is a prime factor in limiting the amount of sickness in your cattery by controlling airborne viruses.

Cleanliness   Your cattery should be kept immaculate, with a strict cleaning and disinfecting program implemented on a regular schedule. Plan to spend at least 20 minutes per cat per day cleaning, to maintain a good standard of health for your cats. Environment is the most critical area for a happy cat and a happy cat is a healthy cat.

Shots   All cats entering your facility should be current on their inoculations and the customer should provide proof of such. You might also request that the owner provide a veterinarian's "certificate of health" on the cat.

KENNELING DOGS

Much thought, planning, and design goes into building a kennel to house dogs. Before you plan your kennel, consider these factors: zoning, laws and ordinances; proximity of your neighbors; proximity of a highway; and the distance from the kennel to your house.

Ventilation System A good ventilation system will consist of a combination of exhaust fans, fresh-air inlets, and your heating system. Additionally, you will want to keep humidity levels low by sealing all cement to promote a much faster drying time.

Drainage You should also allow for proper drainage and plan to have your individual runs slope to an *outside* drain or gutter. Make sure your kennel runs do not slope in such a way that the waste water runs into an adjoining run. You should plan on an average of one drain gutter per 8–10 runs. Minimum 18-inch-high solid dividers should be placed between outside runs; *inside* construction or enclosures should provide each run with total isolation from other runs and animals. All material designed for animal pens should be strong enough to prevent escapes. In addition, all property boundaries should have security fencing installed.

Smoke and Fire Detection System This should be installed and entranceways should be large enough to get your dogs out quickly. If your kennel is located some distance away from your living quarters, you will want to install an alarm system that will also alert you in your home.

Grooming and Food Preparation You should have a separate grooming area and food preparation area. The health of the dogs in your care is very important; you should feed a complete diet, one that is high in nutrition, to promote this good health. Dogs should be groomed and checked for external parasites on a regular basis. Do not exclude preventive dental care from your regular grooming procedure.

Shots All dogs entering your facility should be current on their inoculations and the owner should provide proof of such. Additionally, it is a good idea to request a recent veterinary "health-check" certificate.

BUILDING THE KENNEL

Your proposed building site is important. You must be acutely aware of the proximity of the neighbors' property lines. You must also figure on the distance for a tolerable noise level. The site's appearance and public convenience will also be factors to consider when making your selection. Many people are somewhat apprehensive about leaving their pets at a boarding facility that is located directly on a busy highway. Additionally, the building should be on ground that is high and dry in order to ensure dry kennels, allow for easy drainoff, and keep humidity low.

Outside runs should be built in an east-west direction to enable sunlight to reach them in the winter months. North-sided runs get little sun and greater winds. If building in an area noted for cold climate you should avoid runs that extend out from the north side of your kennel building. The opposite holds true if building in dry or hot climates.

The flooring of your runs can be either cement or gravel. Cement is easier to clean and disinfect; however, gravel is better for dogs' feet. All runs should have a top to prevent dogs from climbing or escaping. The fencing you use in your runs should also surround the kennel area and, as a preventive measure, your entire property line. Gates should have tamper-resistant (dog-proof) locks or latches.

Interior systems should allow for proper ventilation, heating, and air conditioning. If your kennel is located in a cold climate you might consider installing radiant heat in the floor of your outside runs. This eliminates the problem of snow or ice removal in the winter and also keeps the animals warmer and dryer.

All materials used in your kennel building should be strong enough to withstand constant cleaning, disinfecting and hosing.

DAILY OPERATIONS

Your kennel must operate on a strict sanitation program. You must keep all surfaces, and even the air, free of germs. All cleaning products used must be environmentally safe. Check with your veterinarian for a disinfectant that has proven non-hazardous to animals.

To ensure the safety and health of the animals under your care you should feed healthy, complete diets and provide plenty of fresh water. Additionally, never allow an animal to enter your boarding facility without proof of inoculations.

Records should be kept on all business activities. Accurate bookkeeping is essential to running a smooth and profitable business. Accounts must be maintained on a daily basis. Contracts should be made to protect your business against lawsuits resulting from such things as illness, accidental injury or acts of God. Insurance is a must!!! Fire, smoke, and security alarms should be installed. If the

Pet's Name _Sophie_   **Age** _5 years_

Breed _Keeshond_

Day In _1-5_   **Day Out** _1-12_

Medications _None_

Diet _Regular_

Special Instructions/Comments

Sophie gets a cookie every night and a vitamin every morning. Sophie is very well-behaved and likes to have her ears scratched!

Sample kennel card (to be placed outside of housing unit).

kennel building is located some distance from your living quarters, the alarms should be installed to sound in your home also.

Remember to always treat every animal with respect and tender loving care. You are working for them!

Employment Opportunities

KENNEL ASSISTANT

Many large private, show, and boarding kennels/catteries are in desperate need of reliable help. This is the ideal job for those of you who love working with animals yet do not like working with the public. Working with animals is very rewarding, but also very exhausting. Prepare yourself!

A kennel assistant's duties include the following:

1. *Cleaning indoor/outdoor runs.* This includes the removal of all debris (sticks, food, et cetera). It is usually followed by hosing down the runs with a high-powered hose and disinfecting solution. Some facilities prefer to use bleach as it is very effective against numerous bacteria as well as viruses. I strongly advise you to discuss any disinfectant choice with your veterinarian first before using it around animals. A good cleaning and disinfecting routine is necessary and must be done to ensure a healthy environment and restrict the spread of disease.

Kennel assistants play a major role in providing good care.

2. *Feeding and watering* all animals. Animals' dishes should be collected and thoroughly cleaned after every feeding. Water dishes should be kept clean and fresh water should be available at all times.

3. *Grooming*, if required. This is usually minimal, as most show-kennel owners prefer grooming done themselves, or by a professional. (Coat condition is extremely important to the show dog or cat.)

4. *Medicating and worming* (as necessary).

5. *Cleaning and disinfecting* cages, crates, equipment and litter trays.

6. *Bathing*, dental care, and periodic checking for external parasites (fleas, ticks, ringworm).

7. *Exercising* pets.

8. *Security and safety.* To ensure the safety of all animals and deter an escape or possible injury to an animal, always make sure all gates and doors are closed tightly and securely locked, even if you plan on only being gone a moment! This precaution cannot be stressed enough.

Yes, the majority of your time will be spent cleaning, disinfecting, and cleaning again . . . and again . . . and again!

NOTE

A couple of kind words and a few scratches behind the ear can mean so much to a pet who spends most of the time isolated from human companionship. The animal will soon be anxiously awaiting your arrival! This is part of what makes the job rewarding.

To Get the Job

Send a resumé (as outlined in "Pet Shop Employee") to all private, show, and boarding kennels in your area. Many pet publications carry breeder ads in the back of the magazine. Breed clubs also have membership lists available. Additionally, your local veterinarian or yellow pages may be able to supply names of kennel owners in your area.

CONSULTANT—KENNEL BUILDING AND DESIGN

You can make a living as a design consultant for the building of kennels and catteries, or you can expand on your already existing pet-related business by adding this as a side business.

Now, you do not have to spend the next five years majoring in drafting and building design! I am specifically referring to consultation. Your clients will depend on you for valuable advice in the designing stage of their proposed kennel or cattery. Your professional input will help your clients to plan a more efficient and practical kennel or cattery. In addition to designing kennels and catteries, you can also develop a consulting service for existing boarding, private, or show kennels, as well as veterinary or animal care facilities.

Basically, anyone can design an efficient and practical kennel or cattery, and almost anyone can learn how to successfully operate one. All this knowledge is readily available in the many books available on kennel and cattery building and management. Numerous publications cover every aspect from the smallest design detail to the everyday operation once the building is erected. You can

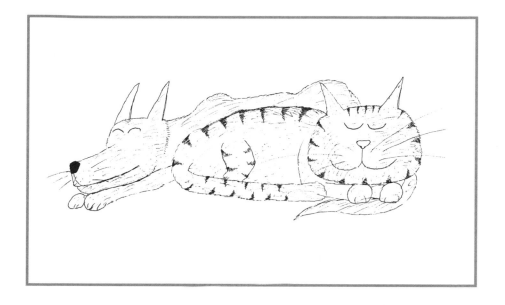

Conscientious kennel owners know how to provide the proper size housing no matter who the tenants are.

easily learn how to plan, design, and operate any kennel or cattery by doing a little investigating in pet trade magazines and in your local library.

When designing a kennel or cattery for a client, you must first learn for what purpose the building will be used. Will it primarily be used as a facility for cats or dogs? For boarding or as a private kennel or cattery? If it will be privately owned, what size is the breed that will be the primary occupants? Will the facility be open to the public? Will it mainly be an animal shelter or a health-care facility?

Your next step will be to determine the size of the proposed structure, as well as the required number of enclosures. Get a budget range figure from your clients for this. If you are well acquainted with various designs and know the approximate cost of materials and contractors, you can design an efficient working plan for the clients that is within their budget range.

The following is a quick checklist to use in planning design and layout for your own or a client's kennel, with considerations that are important for both boarding and private facilities.

- Proper zoning
- Gutters/drains
- Soil testing
- Drainage systems
- Waste management
- Sanitation/hose locations
- Geographical layout
- Sun, shade, and wind factors
- Electricity
- Noise level factor
- Plumbing
- Foundation
- Heating/air conditioning
- Isolation area
- Food preparation area
- Air circulation/exhaust fans
- Fire prevention
- Sink/tub area
- Alarm systems
- Grooming room
- Security fencing
- Wall caging units, or banks
- Indoor/outdoor runs
- Exercise area
- Cleaning and disinfecting plan
- Wall and flooring material
- Mode of operation
- Reception area
- Accounting, bookkeeping
- Safety practices and prevention

CONSULTANT—KENNEL MANAGEMENT

Plan for Success

In order to secure new customers, you should be able to prepare a plan of operation that will promote success in their already existing business and in newly established businesses.

Such a plan should show detailed information on designing for efficiency, safety precautions, material specifications, sanitation and drainage, and kennel design, as well as presenting a detailed plan for successful management. There are also many reasons why an already established kennel or cattery might seek your professional consultation services. For instance, their present boarding business may be losing money or faltering, or they may feel that they are not earning to their top potential. They may consistently encounter sickness in a private or show establishment or they may need to learn a more time-efficient daily routine. The list can go on and on; however, all you really need to know is how to devise a successful business plan for these clients.

A successful business plan for kennel management should include the following:

- Everyday management
- Basic business plan
- Bookkeeping/record keeping
- Price index
- Profit and loss statement
- Daily operation routine
- Disease prevention
- Marketing/advertising
- Improving client relations
- Improving employee efficiency
- Adding a sales floor/retail area

- Daily management
- Preventive medicine/ nutritional advice
- Proper exercise program
- Proper feeding programs
- Cleaning/disinfecting
- Improving sales/retail stock

- Seasonal forecasts
- Loss prevention
- Cost efficiency and cost control
- "Boarding release" and other standard kennel forms and agreements

Acquiring Customers

Send direct-mail inquiries to members of boarding and kennel associations, kennel clubs, breed clubs, handlers' associations, and grooming organizations.

Design an informative and attractive brochure which tells the potential customer how they will *benefit directly* from your services. You can save them money and time by designing a more efficient business plan. Your services will help the client generate more income through a proven marketing program designed specifically for boarding kennels. Make sure your brochure or packet looks professional and gives you the appearance of being a successful businessperson. Remember that nothing sells better than success! Contact a good list company and inquire about renting a mailing list of boarding kennels and related interests.

Make sure to keep an ad in all pet publications to secure new clients who are still in the planning and pre-building stage. Additionally, you should post notices at pet shops and veterinary clinics and rent a trade booth or show space at cat or dog shows and pet industry trade shows and expos.

2

Opening a Pet Supply Shop

There is nothing greater than being your own boss! Nothing, however, involves more responsibilities than owning and operating your own business. If you believe that you can run a small business successfully, and enjoy the idea of being self-employed while working with pets and the public, then you probably have what it takes to own a pet shop.

First, I would suggest that you enroll in a small-business course at your local college where you will acquire information invaluable to operating a small business. This information will include bookkeeping, market research, accounting, estimating your profits, business analysis, handling profit and loss statements, and other general information specifically geared to small-business ownership.

Opening a Pet Shop

A pet shop is a business that supplies goods related to the care of pets. Your pet shop might be a simple, family-run neighborhood business, or it could be an innovative and complete one-stop service shop, including, but not limited to, a retail store, boarding facility, veterinary clinic, grooming, therapeutic spas and perhaps the sale of a few healthy pets. Whatever your business will be, you must preplan it down to the smallest detail *before* you open!

Consider just *some* of your opening costs:

- Fixtures
- Sales tax deposit
- Stock
- Contracting
- Rent or lease
- Design

- Licensing/permits
- Phone/utilities
- Utility deposit
- Insurance

- Lease deposit
- Advertising
- Legal fees
- Supplies and miscellaneous costs

....

Good financial backing is a necessity for opening a pet shop! Additionally, it is not a good idea to seek financial assistance through a professional institution. All funds should ideally be provided by you; after all, you do not want to open your store already in debt! When purchasing interior fixtures and necessities, you can make do with the basics. Buying things that are too elaborate can be an awful waste of money. There will be plenty of time later for improvements and business additions.

THE SHOP ITSELF

The location of the shop is very important to your success. Ideally, your shop should be situated for easy access in a high-traffic area. If possible, you should be near an anchor store (as in a mall or strip center) that does a good, brisk business. Being close to a veterinary clinic is very promising, as you will have a higher concentration of pet owners within easy access to your store.

Malls may have higher rents but they draw many more customers than a shop situated elsewhere. Most mall leases will have expenses in addition to regular rent. These expenses will include your portion of the shared mall maintenance sometimes known as "CAM," or Common

Area Maintenance. This includes parking, snow removal, sweeping and floor upkeep, and so on. It ranges from approximately $.50 to $5.00 per square foot. Other mall expenses are advertising (your percentage of the mall promotion), insurance, and your percent of the real estate taxes (an amount usually equal to "CAM"). In addition to charging a basic rental fee, a few malls also charge a *percentage* rent—that is, an additional rent surcharge due on a percentage of your sales.

You may wish to give your pet shop a "theme," such as a jungle or safari atmosphere. Complete the "theme" with real or artificial trees and plants, piped-in music or pre-recorded sounds of animals in the wild. Gimmicks like these work well in attracting potential customers to your establishment, as many will visit your store just to see its attractive displays.

A GOOD BUSINESS PLAN

A good business plan is essential to success! You probably think you know everything there is to know about your proposed pet shop. After all, that's all you've been thinking about for months, possibly years! However, with a good business plan you'll be surprised to learn that you didn't know your prospective business as well as you thought! A good business plan will give you a much better insight to opening and operating your retail establishment.

Most pet shops' initial investment starts at around $50,000. Your average monthly operating expense will be around $8500 and this figure will vary in accordance with the number of employees in your store, your "draw" (owner's salary), the cost of replenishing the store's inventory and available stock, plus any payments on bank loans or to investors you may have dealt with in obtaining your start-up costs or initial capital.

Remember: Knowing everything about pets is enough for the hobbyist but does not a business run! You must be able to manage your *business. Maintaining proper cash records is essential to good management.* This includes daily cash receipts, cash disbursements, monthly income and balance sheets, accounts payable and organized inventory and/or purchase records.

Again, I would suggest that you enroll in some business courses at your local college before investing any money in your proposed pet shop. After all, you would not purchase a new car if you did not know how to operate one, would you? So why would you invest a much greater amount of money in purchasing a new business if you don't know how to operate it?

Take a look a the following business plan outline:

Name of Business   What will you name your business? Will it be a catchy name, or will you use your own name? Have you registered your name and checked to make sure no other business is using that name?

Business History   What is the history of this business? When was it established? How has its concept matured? Has business fluctuated or been steady? If it has fluctuated, what was the reason? What has been the area competition, and how has it fared?

Business Summary   Describe your business, its goals, the products you will carry, the services you will offer. What will make your business unique? How will your business benefit the customers?

Management and Owner Qualifications What are your past experiences and qualifications for operating your new business? Who will work with you? What are their qualifications?

Opening Preparation Have you checked into zoning and licenses? What about your location? What are your contracting needs? Will you need additional electrical or water output for your marine department?

Operating Plan What are your store hours, and complaint and return policies? What is your daily work schedule? How will the daily work get done and by whom? From which suppliers will you purchase merchandise to stock your store?

Financial Plan This should include a one-year sales and expense forecast and one-year cash flow figures. You should have a balance sheet, which will tell you the business' assets and debts, and the financial investments of its backers or stockholders (you). List your opening costs. Profit and loss statements give you your best insight into your shop's weaknesses.

Market Research Who are your customers? What is their average income range? Who is your competition, and how will you differ from your competition to gain your share of the market?

Marketing Plan Marketing is the backbone of your business! A successful marketing plan plays a key role in your business success. A poorly devised marketing program will only result in empty bank accounts and poor sales. You should definitely take a course in marketing, or read as many marketing books as possible, *before* you open your business. A good, strong marketing plan is the air that your business will breathe.

Advertising How will you advertise? Will you need a name, slogan or motto? What service will you offer that will make you stand out above your present competition? What about specials, sales and other promotion plans? You can increase store sales by offering special deals such as free fish with the purchase of a tank setup, or free food with the purchase of a hamster. What about advertising costs? Will certain ads draw more customers than others? What kinds of advertising vehicles are available for you? What is your business statement? How do you want to "position" your business in your community?

Diversification You should also consider diversifying as a means to supplement your store's income. I strongly advocate the second-business strategy; any move that will bring more customers into your store is sure to boost sales. Some second-business or additional-service ideas are pet search services, grooming, boarding, animal identification tattooing, and aquarium maintenance services. You can also diversify on your "service" itself. This means to offer some variation from your traditional service—for instance, by offering a kind of first-class service. This could be the availability of phone-in service: The busy customer phones in his or her order(s) for pet food or other goods in your store, then simply pulls up in front of your store, and an employee rushes out with the order. A convenience like this is sure to attract busy people who work long hours, as well as the handicapped, the elderly, and affluent customers who have come to expect first-class service from the businesses they patronize.

Customer Relations Your most important business practice is good customer relations. Make your customer the most important part of your business! After all, the customer *is* your business. Treat your customer honestly; supply correct and accurate information on all products and pets; be kind, courteous and, above all, respectful. By following these guidelines, you will have customers who will return time and again, and confidently refer you to others, and you will build a business that will have a good, reliable name in the community. Establish yourself with a respectable reputation from the beginning, and you will be successful for years.

The more prepared you are *before* you enter into business, the more likely your chances for success. Take some business courses at your local college, plan your business down to the doorstop at your shop's entrance, and devise a good solid marketing plan. Do your homework! Then sit back, pat yourself on the back, and watch your perfectly planned business grow and grow!

ON THE INSIDE—KEY MARKETING TOOLS

Your success in this business is a unique combination of several factors:

1. Business managing capabilities (yours and/or your employees')
2. Promotional marketing and advertising success
3. Knowledge of the products you carry
4. Knowledge of the services and pets you offer
5. Knowledge of your competitors and what products they sell
6. Your treatment of your customers

7. Your "uniqueness." What you do to make your business stand out from the others. The services and merchandise you have to offer and how you present these goods to your customers.
8. Luck. (Don't rely on this one too much!)

All the preceding can be put into one neat little package that spells S-U-C-C-E-S-S!

Let's focus now on how your store presents itself to your customers. You can be the sweetest, nicest, most knowledgeable person in the world, but if your store is a mess, or understocked or understaffed, no customer will stick around long enough to find out! What message is your store sending to your customers? To find out, become your own customer! That's right. Pretend you are a customer: Leave your store, then reenter and pretend you're looking at it through your customer's eyes.

As you walk in, what does your store entrance say to you? Is your entrance large, open and inviting? Is it blocked by boxes, store pets, sales items or other clutter? Continue on into the store. How does it smell? This is the first thing your customers will notice. Some odors that you should be sensitive to are animal litter, soiled shavings, old food, wet dogs, the stagnant smell of standing turtle water or foul fish tank water, and animal urine. If you notice an odor problem, locate its source and eliminate the problem the best that you can. This may mean that you have to clean 20 gerbil cages, change all the litter trays, or scrub down the rabbit hutches. This does not mean spraying a scented room freshener to mask the odor! Keep your shop clean; stock only effective, reliable, safe products; and sell only healthy pets.

What is your first impression of the store? Does it have a theme that creates an interesting and inviting atmosphere. Is the design appealing? Is the climate of your store comfortable? Are the aisles and walkways clean and clear of stock? Are the shelves stocked according to department, and is this arrangement convenient (are your fish food and supplies adjacent to your aquarium displays)? Is your visible merchandise clean and dust-free, and is this stock rotated? Are your signs clean and neat or frayed and worn?

Are your in-store displays designed to draw the customers' attention and make them take notice of merchandise displayed? What about your lighting? Is it either too dim or too bright? Are your windows and displays clear enough from excess signs to create an open feeling in your store? Windows that are too cluttered diminish the amount of sunlight and create a gloomy, closed-in atmosphere. Are your employees well-groomed and neatly dressed? Are they knowledgeable and pleasant? Do they offer the customer assistance?

GETTING THE MOST OUT
OF YOUR EMPLOYEES

There are a few guidelines that will result in maximum production from your employees. For instance, if you tell an employee to rearrange the leashes before lunch and you then walk away, odds are that on your return you will find that the job has not been done anywhere near the way you had expected. However, as easy as it would seem to just do it yourself, *don't*! That's why you have employees! By following three simple steps, you should find delegating responsibilities a fearless task:

1. Make sure your employee is capable of doing the task. If your employees haven't been properly trained in tank cleaning, don't expect them to get the job done properly.

2. Question your employee about the job you have assigned. For instance, you may have instructed an employee to move some bird toys to an endcap display to promote an upcoming sale. You then ask the employee if he/she understands. "Yep." Okay, great! But later, when you check on the employee's progress, you learn he/she has spent almost an hour moving heavy bags of birdseed to the endcap! What a birdbrain! You *asked* whether the employee understood when you assigned the task! What happened? The fault lies with you. Instead of asking the employee whether he/she understood, you should have said, "Now, tell me, what you are going to do, and how long do you think this project will take?"

3. Make sure your employees understand that they can come to you. Let them know that you are more than happy to explain something in more detail or assist in other ways if needed. Your employees should feel comfortable in approaching you with problems and discussing possible solutions with you.

Continued training, encouraging "pep" talks, and acknowledgment and recognition of their achievements all are essential to successful employee management.

ATTRACTING CUSTOMER TRAFFIC

What observation have you made on your customer traffic? Watch and find out which areas of the store are most heavily traveled. If you find you have a low-traffic area with merchandise that is getting buried, rotate this merchandise to a higher-traffic area, or bring a popular item into the low-traffic area.

Don't keep the same displays up too long, as your old customers might become bored with them and seek out a more interesting place to shop. Frequently change your endcaps, or set up amusing and unique displays. Keep it interesting! Add some clever and witty signs. Make the customer take notice with humorous sayings on your pet cages. Listen (eavesdrop!) to your customers to see what areas of your store spark their interest and what areas bore them into a conversation about Aunt Martha's back problems.

ONCE THEY'RE IN, DO THEY BUY?

To increase sales in your store, you should make your displays as irresistible as possible. For instance, to increase fish sales, you might try using red backdrops for black fish, or Dalmatian Mollys with white or pearlescent artificial plants and backdrops and gravel of hot pink. Sharks display well in natural "tankscapes" with backgrounds of sea blue, natural gravel, attractive rocks and green plants. Black fish are beautiful against gold backgrounds! Use your imagination. Place one white kitten in with a litter of black kittens, or vice versa.

Anything that will make your merchandise stand out to capture your customers' attention is sure to promote sales. Offering "pet starter kits" with the purchase of a rabbit, for instance, will appeal to the customer. These kits might include a bag of feed, watering tube, food dish and toy, along with a booklet you have prepared on rabbit care. Offering aquarium setup packages (tank, filter, pump, heater, gravel, hood and light) for a discounted price (over buying each item separately) might boost sales in this department. Go ahead and throw in the first three fish for free!

To encourage the sales of your really slow movers, or dust collectors as some would call them, place them in a heavy-traffic or high-visibility area (usually up front by the check-out counter), and run a special red-tag sale on them. Another method to move those "non-movers" is to offer them in a package deal, such as offering an artificial aquarium plant free or half-price with the purchase of a goldfish or aquarium gravel.

Keep your checkout area free from excess clutter, and make sure that customers cannot see the "back" of your displays, so they do not feel that they have seen all there is to see and it is now time to leave the store.

ATTENTION GRABBERS

Some other methods of promoting your shop include what I like to call "AdSOS"—for example, advertising 60-second commercial spots on local radio stations at peak times. Additionally, you may advertise in local newspapers.

To test the effectiveness of your ads, use coupons in ads that the customer will have to bring into the store. Distribute coupon books through grocery stores, kennels, grooming shops, veterinary clinics or pet shows. Set up a booth display at a local pet show. Offer free educational demonstrations on products or pet care at local schools, malls, fairs or community events. Create a discount club or preferred-customer cards.

Sponsor local events, tournaments or competitions.

For more information on marketing for a successful business, please see chapter 16.

THREE "PARROTS PLUS PETS" DOLLARS

$3 $3

$ SAVE $

On any brand dry dog food 25lb. or larger

Expires March 21, 1999

$3 $3

Using a coupon in your ad will attract attention and demand a response.

IN THE PUBLIC EYE

Your store has another image to maintain also—that is, as a respectable member of the business community. Be sure your store plays an active role in publicly (and privately) supporting groups such as the local humane society and animal welfare organizations. Your support goes a long way, and as a pet shop owner, you have an ethical obligation to support these animal welfare groups and associations. This support will also earn you added respect as a merchant and a person, giving your personal, professional and public image an additional healthy boost.

OPENING A SECOND STORE

Opening a second shop will probably entail more time and energy than you expect, so you should have a reliable person who is capable of running the first shop in your absence. This person should be able to work well with customers, tend to any livestock, operate the business, and be trusted to handle money.

Once your store is well under way, it is pertinent that it not rely financially on your original store. If circumstances beyond your control force the old store to close, both stores would then collapse.

Ideally, the location of your new shop should be as far away from your original store as possible. You want the opportunity to attract as new customers those residents you haven't be able to reach in your original shop's location. And why go into competition with yourself?!

ADDING A SECOND BUSINESS TO THE SHOP

Business diversification is an excellent means to increase your income. Even if your pet shop is still in the planning stage, it's never too early to consider additional avenues that may generate more income. Diversification can drastically increase your income while allowing your overhead to remain virtually the same. I strongly advocate the addition of a second business *adjacent* to your pet shop. It is ideal for drawing more customers into your business establishment. The following sections provide some suggestions for a second business.

Petting Zoo

A day at the farm! What could be more fun for youngsters? Petting zoos can be a great way to attract more customers to your pet store, as visitors will most likely visit the pet shop afterward!

However, there are many *major* negatives to adding a petting zoo. You must consider the amount of property you have available; you may not have sufficient grounds for a petting zoo. Additionally, you will need to consider the costs of erecting farm buildings, and caring for and sheltering the animals.

Do local ordinances and zoning laws allow a petting zoo? Who will take care of the animals? Who will maintain the grounds and oversee the admission of guests? Also, do not forget the additional insurance! The animals in your petting zoo should be immaculate, well-cared-for at all times, and selected for health and temperament. Sheep, lambs, goats, llamas, miniature pigs, cows, chickens, ducks, geese, turkeys, rabbits, ponies and miniature horses, chinchillas, ferrets, guinea pigs, hamsters, gerbils, mice, rats, lizards, toads, frogs and snakes are just some of the possible candidates. Be sure your zoo has an area for resting, and add some simple playground equipment for children to release some of their energy. Pony rides would be great, too! Top it all off with an attractive stone walk and some park benches.

Above all else, take excellent care of the animals! Feed them healthy diets, supply fresh water, and provide adequate shelter. They should have easy access to shade and a warm place to escape from winter's cold. *Do not place any of your animals in a situation where they might experience abuse or mishandling from visitors.* Include a good, correct "preventative medicine" program, recommended by your veterinarian, in the care of your farm animals.

Library

To "beef-up" sales and attract more customers, add a library room where visitors may check out information and educational material. This includes breed books; how-to books on care and training; and informational video tapes on different breeds, their care, training and grooming. In addition, you may wish to include a section of fictional material, especially for the children.

Do not forget to stock your library with books on all species of pets, such as fish, birds, reptiles, horses, gerbils, hamsters, ferrets, guinea pigs and rabbits. A small checkout fee *may* be charged to cover your costs; however, I do not recommend it. After all, your customers can check out much of this material free at the local library. This is a good reason to carry a more in-depth selection than the library does, especially on dogs and cats. Remember, your main objective is to get the customer to visit your store! Make it a practice to stock material that is not available at your local library. This will help ensure that customers come to your store to locate the material they need.

Video Rental

The major benefit in renting videos is to increase your customers' educational awareness. This helps keep them returning to your store, as the videos get them more interested in their pet or hobby and therefore more aware of the products you carry. (Many videos are sponsored by the pet-products industry.) Customers return and buy the products introduced in the videos! If you wish, you can rent your videos for a little more than your local video store rents theirs, as you are not in direct competition with the same videos that these stores carry. You should be able to charge a $3.00–$4.00 rental fee for videos.

Newsletter

A monthly or bimonthly shop newsletter may be a novel approach to attract customers. Give your newsletter a catchy name, and have fun with the design. Possibly, sponsor a contest to name the newsletter, with a gift certificate for store merchandise as the prize(s).

There are many terrific programs available for your computer that will enable you to make a professionally designed and attractive newsletter.

Each issue should be loaded with coupons good for discounts on such things as birdseed, fish and fish supplies, small animal supplies, grooming products or other goods available in your shop. You might also run specials on other services that you offer such as nail clipping, wing clipping, small animal boarding, grooming, teeth cleaning and aquarium maintenance.

Also include local pet news, special features that focus on customers and their pets, the latest information on health care, and product updates. New product information and reviews will help promote particular products and give your sales an added boost. These product promotions can run with special sales of these items.

It is also a good idea to sell advertising or coupon space to local groomers, boarding kennels, breeders or veterinarians. You can generate additional income by inserting a classified section in the back of your newsletter. This section might contain headings for "new or used" pet-related equipment for sale, "wanted" ads or "services offered."

You can obtain a customer mailing list by asking all customers who come into your shop if they would like to be on your mailing list. Explain to the customer that you have a newsletter that contains invaluable information on pet care and pet care products, plus additional coupons good on products and services that you and other local businesses offer. More simply, you could leave a stack of newsletters next to the checkout area, with a sign that reads "Please help yourself to a FREE copy of our Newsletter." *If* you charge a nominal subscription fee for your newsletter, explain to your customers that although there is a small subscription fee, each issue contains many valuable coupons worth far more than the subscription price.

Other Possibilities

Other ideas for second businesses are pet identification (there are several forms, such as tattooing), lost pet recovery, grooming, pet referral services, feed sales, aquarium maintenance and leasing services, nail clipping, teeth cleaning and wing clipping.

Specialty feed sales is an especially good idea because customers will return regularly for more of the specific brand of food they use. Besides, with these, you will not have competition from the supermarket. Your feed should be located in the back of your store so that customers will have to "browse" through your store each and every time they return for more feed.

Free services that require customers to enter your store also increase traffic on your sales floor. Some ideas for free services are aquarium water testing, wing clipping and nail clipping.

Diversifying means letting your imagination go! Find a void in the marketplace and fill it! Your customers will appreciate the added "special services" that you offer, and you, in return, will find an increase in your overall profits!

Exotic Pet Shop

Are you a herpetologist? Do you enjoy watching and studying these fascinating animals? Do you keep any reptiles or amphibians as pets or for a hobby? If so, then your

Birds like the Amazon parrot are one type of pet benefiting from pet identification and recovery systems.

knowledge might make you well suited for a herpetile specialty pet shop.

Are you drawn to the extraordinary, novel or eccentric pet? Many people enjoy having the unusual for pets; this is why uncommon or rare pets do not remain rare for long.

There is no doubt that reptiles are the pets of the future. Their popularity is gaining every day. New books on these animals' care are being published with more frequency. Herpetarium displays are becoming more common in pet stores. More and more hobbyists each year buy these animals for pets. Herpetiles are easy to care for, take up very little space, and are amazingly fun to watch. They are also readily accepted by most landlords who will not allow cats or dogs. They are less expensive to feed than are most pets, and there are almost limitless exotic designs for their housing units.

HERPETILES

If you select this retail specialty, you must *know* herpetiles. You need to know the proper diet for each species you intend to carry, and be fully knowledgeable about medications, parasites, and monitored environmental-temperature control. You should be aware that herpetiles are cold-blooded animals and that many will not breed unless they have gone through a period of hibernation. Are you also aware that hibernation occurs during specific changes of temperature, light and humidity and that each species has different requirements for these conditions? (Most will rely on cycles similar to their natural habitat.) Here are a few selections for your reptile sales:

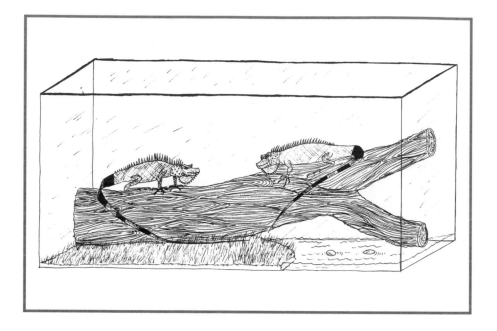

Herpetiles take up very little room and are amazingly
fun to watch.

Turtles   Painted, sliders, soft-shell and box.

Amphibians   Tree frogs, green frogs, fire-belly toads,
tiger salamanders and water dogs. Most American and/or
marine toads.

Lizards   Anoles (chameleons), iguanas (green and
spiny), savannah monitors, curly tails, swifts, skinks,
amevias and, possibly, tegus.

Snakes   Rat, water and garter snakes. Small common
boa constrictors, Burmese pythons, king snakes.

Others   Other exotic species may include tarantulas, black scorpions and land crabs.

Find good, knowledgeable suppliers for your herpetiles. You will want a supplier who consisently offers a good selection of *healthy* animals at fair prices. *You may need to use different wholesalers to obtain the best of each species.* Local herp breeders, hobbyists and collectors may often be your best providers.

Immediately after your animals arrive, check them for external parasites and disease. Check ears and armpits for ticks. Run a white cloth over your snakes, and examine the cloth for evidence of mite infestation. Look for raw noses or mouth rot. Let your supplier know, from the very start, that you most definitely will not accept any animal that is not in top condition. Additionally, each animal that comes into your store should receive a routine worming.

Always keep a record on each animal you receive. This valuable record should contain the name of the supplier, wholesaler or breeder from whom the animal came; its condition upon arrival; the overall health of the animal; plus your cost. These records will be a great help when it comes time to reorder.

Keep all reptiles immaculately clean! House each species in an attractive yet *suitable* environment. Feed a healthy diet. For example, coat your crickets with powdered vitamins before using them as feed. Always feed your animals before your shop opens, *or* after closing, and *always* have fresh water available. Having healthier specimens results in better sales, more customer referrals, and repeat customers. You should also work with a good veterinarian, one who is knowledgeable regarding herpetiles.

Keep all reptiles immaculately clean, and be sure they have a healthy diet.

OPENING A PET SUPPLY SHOP

KNOW YOUR CUSTOMER

You will find that you have two distinctly different types of customers: the expert or professional herpetologist, and the average customer.

The professionals are an important part of your business. Not only will they rely on you for supplies, but they will encourage new customers to visit your store. What about the average customer, the "browser"? They are just as important! Odds are, with every one herpetile purchase, fifty more will result! Most will return for another animal, or housing equipment, and almost all will return, time and again, for their feed and supplies. Rarely will customers fail to return after their initial purchase. Where else will they find that special diet needed to maintain their new pet?

You must know how to care properly for each and every species you plan to sell, and your customers will expect you to pass this information on to them. Consider preparing a mini pamphlet on each species you carry, to give customers with their purchase. These pamphlets should include each particular species' history, housing information and proper health care, along with accurate feeding instructions to maintain a healthy and balanced diet. Other topics you might want to include in your pamphlet are environmental control; the heating, humidity and light cycles for the species; information regarding external and internal parasites; and any particularities common to that breed (such as shedding skin). Make sure your pamphlet has your store name, address and phone number printed clearly on the cover so that the customer will be able to contact you quickly and easily if necessary.

Your store should also be able to provide the proper diet, housing needs, equipment and supplies for each species you sell. Your herpetile accessory display should always be well-stocked and kept up-to-date and in season. Many supplies are seasonal, as you will learn, and many are in more demand than others. Time will give you the experience and knowledge needed to determine what stock moves faster or is in greater demand.

Give your customers a huge selection of supplies, a wide variety of feed, sound professional advice and top-quality service, and you will gain loyal customers who will return for many years to come.

GETTING STARTED

You should be able to start in a limited space. If you open the business in a portion of your home, check local laws, ordinances and *zoning*.

It would be more advisable to rent a small shop in a heavy-traffic area, such as near a mall or busy intersection. Perhaps more important than location is *marketing. Advertising should be your top priority when starting a business.* Public awareness is the only way to achieve success in business! You may have the best prices, the finest selection of goods, and offer quality service; however, all this means nothing if the customers don't know you're there! Heavy advertising is of the utmost importance when opening your store.

You will need to send advertisements to every paper in your serviceable area. Because your store carries a unique stock, it is quite logical to advertise broadly; customers will most likely travel greater distances to purchase what they are unable to get in their own neighborhood. Keep in mind what I stated previously regarding returning customers: " . . . for each sale you make, many more will result!" As you establish a regular clientele, your advertising costs will be reduced greatly, with the need for only an occasional sale notice and a listing in the yellow pages.

I wish you the greatest luck with your exotic/herpetile shop. I know you can make it a success!!!

Pet Shop Employee

Don't want the responsibility of ownership? Try being a pet shop employee. Not many career choices can equal the joy of working with animals; they are precious! Working in a pet shop entitles you to care for these precious creatures, while at the same time giving you the opportunity to work with people and learn the retail business. By working closely with the public, you will have the opportunity to meet many different people, and pet shop clients are happy! What brings children greater joy than buying toys for a new puppy, selecting new fish for an aquarium, or picking out a furry little hamster? It's shopping the whole family will enjoy, and they will rely on you time and again for professional advice and product information. This means you must be up-to-date on all products your store carries, know the different kinds of animals, be aware of and recognize fish diseases, and give advice on grooming requirements and immunizations.

YOUR JOB

Among your duties, you will be expected to do the following:

1. Take care of the pets offered for sale. This includes cleaning and feeding. These chores are usually done early in the morning, before the store is opened, with an occasional cleanup during the day. You will be expected to keep all cages, tanks and pens sanitary, and all animals well-cared-for, with fresh water available at all times.

2. Keep shelves stocked and set up displays. It will be your job to make sure that the pet shop radiates a clean, appealing appearance.

3. Help customers with product selection. This is where you really need the knowledge! You must know everything from pets to flea products, aquarium heaters and birdseed! There are many good pet industry and pet trade publications available that will keep you abreast of new and current pet products.

4. Ring up sales, handle minor problems, help with inventory, and be involved in loss prevention.

FINDING EMPLOYMENT

When seeking employment in a pet shop, your first step is to send a resumé to the store. Your resumé should include all experience you may have had in working with animals.

It should also include any sales or marketing background you might have.

Be sure to stress any experience you have had that has placed you in direct contact with the public. It might help if you add (in your resumé) your love for animals and your knowledge regarding the different breeds of fish, birds, reptiles and small animals (guinea pigs, hamsters, rabbits, gerbils, mice, rats and ferrets). Send your resumé to all the pet shops in your local area. Always follow up on your resumé with a visit to the shop, or a phone call requesting an interview, if possible.

Salaries differ and may depend on the size of the store, the amount of business the store does and, of course, your experience and job performance. If you are considering a business move to ownership of a pet shop, *I strongly suggest you work as an employee first.*

3

Grooming Options

Professional Groomer

....

There are several reasons for entering the grooming profession—namely, a love for animals, the advantages of self-employment, the opportunity for additional income and the convenience of working from your home. In addition, the benefits and rewards that each animal will receive, through your special care, make this a career you can be proud of. The result of your grooming will be evident in each animal, for they will leave you as happier, healthier pets.

Many of today's groomers are self-taught; others have learned grooming under an apprenticeship program; and still others have attended a trade school that specializes in grooming. I strongly recommend that you *enroll in a trade school* where you will receive the best training and instruction available. Be patient; it will take some time to learn how to properly groom the many different breeds!

WHAT IS GROOMING?

Grooming consists of bathing, brushing, combing, nail clipping, ear care, styling, clipping and scissoring. It also may consist of cleaning teeth, expressing the anal glands, defleaing, and deskunking. The entire process can be briefly described in the following manner:

Step 1: It is essential to *brush and comb out* each animal's entire coat before bathing. Wetting a matted or tangled coat only worsens the condition. When brushing and combing, always work on the animal systematically. This means you should start at the hindquarters and work your way toward the head. Starting with the left rear leg, brush and then comb out both the top and the underside of the leg. Move to the right rear leg and repeat. After completion of the rear legs, move to the front legs and, starting with the left leg, repeat the same process. The rest of the body should then be brushed and combed in the following order: tail, left side of body, right side of body, underside, front and chest area, head and ears.

After receiving a groomer's special care, the animal is a happier, healthier pet.

Step 2: After the animal is thoroughly brushed and combed out, the next step is *bathing*. Wet the dog following the same pattern described in "Step 1." Shampoo the dog, and use a rubber bath brush to work the shampoo into the coat. Rinse the dog thoroughly, and wring the water out of the coat. Towel dry the animal, and place in a cage with a dryer. Do not let the coat dry entirely. You will want the coat to be slightly damp for "Step 3."

Step 3: *Blow drying* is essential to give the animal a fluffy coat that is free of kinks and waves. It also diminishes the problem of curly coats or coats that lie too close to the skin. Brush as you blow dry, again working from the hindquarters to the front of the head.

Step 4: *Finish off* your grooming by cleaning the animal's ears, at which time you might check for problems such as ear mites or infection, and also trim the nails.

CATS

Do not forget cats as part of your grooming business. Many groomers limit themselves to just dogs and are therefore missing out on half their potential customers. Cat grooming is slightly different from dog grooming. For example, cats hate to be submerged in water. Bathing a cat is much easier if the cat is held in a sink or washbasin and the coat is wet with a spray hose (soft stream). After wetting the coat, turn off the water and shampoo the entire coat. When the cat is completely washed, turn the water back on and rinse the coat *thoroughly*. Wring the coat out, and wrap the cat in a towel to absorb the excess water.

The use of a cat rack that fits over the edge of a tub, or a screen that fits in the bottom of the sink, can prove to be beneficial when bathing frightened cats. The screen gives the cats a place to sink their claws into (rather than you). Muzzles work well, too. Additionally, you could angle a framed screen in the sink, facing the back wall. The angle of the screen gives the cat a base on which to climb, but without an escape route. Do not angle the screen toward you, as the cat will continue the climb up your body!

Hold a frightened cat by the scruff, or nape, of the neck; this will prevent the cat from sinking its teeth in you. Also, never let your attention be diverted when you are bathing a cat. Cats are fast!

GROOMING FEES

The average grooming cost is $15.00–$30.00 per cat and approximately $15.00–$60.00 per dog, depending on the breed, the condition of the coat, and your grooming shop's location. Grooming fees differ from city to suburbs and from state to state. When establishing your fee, ask yourself the following questions:

Who is my competition?

How do my prices compare? If they are higher, do I offer something special or unique to justify them? If they are lower, can I make a profit?

What are my operating expenses?

Can the present market's economy justify my pricing?

Remember to keep in mind your future grooming business when setting a price. For instance, let's say you now work out of your home, which keeps your overhead low. Therefore, you might think it reasonably safe to assume that you can set your prices lower, right? WRONG! You have to allow for your future expansion plans! Otherwise, you will find upon expansion that you have not set your fees high enough to cover your newly added expenses and overhead. Consequently, you will have to figure out how to raise your fees without losing customers who are accustomed to paying your low prices. In addition to a pre-established base fee, many groomers will charge extra for special services such as dematting, flea dip, special clipping, hot oil treatment and tattooing for permanent identification.

CUSTOMERS

To ensure that clients will return time and again, you must consistently turn out quality work. Above all, you must treat each animal with the best care and attention possible. Nothing will please customers more than to see their pet not only well-groomed but with tail wagging at the sight of the groomer or the sound of the groomer's voice.

I also recommend that you keep a record on each dog or cat that you groom. You should file these records under the owner's last name and the animal's call name. With these cards, you or your employees will be better prepared for any special handling problems or grooming requests when that animal returns. Moreover, these records are invaluable if you are having a slow season, as you can send out gentle reminders (to customers) that their pets are due for a grooming. Sending thank-you cards to each of your customers (or their pets!) is also a great way to add the personal touch that guarantees return customers! It's a terrific, inexpensive way to ensure repeat business and long-standing, faithful customers.

Nothing will please customers more than a well-groomed pet, tail wagging at the sight of the groomer.

NOTE

Grooming may require experience and time to master. Do not feel discouraged if you are a little awkward in the beginning . . . most new groomers are!!! Once you have studied or apprenticed to learned the fundamentals and "tricks of the trade," you will, in time, become a skilled professional groomer.

Moreover, once you have learned how to groom professionally, you can get started right away by grooming from your very own home! You may wish to convert a room, basement, garage or even a small outbuilding on your property into a mini grooming shop. After you have an established client list, you might think about opening your own shop (see the following section, "Grooming Shop").

Grooming Shop

DESIGNING A GROOMING SHOP

The most important components to grooming shop design are electricity, plumbing, heating, air conditioning, ventilation, flooring, fixtures and equipment, office area, reception area and phone system (your phone system should be designed for easy access from various locations in your shop).

Ideally, shampooing and drying areas should be separated from the clipping and styling areas. This arrangement reduces the risk of a misdirected water spray, or air from a dryer interfering with fine scissoring or other styling procedures. Additionally, the air in a shampooing and drying area can be much too hot and humid for successful scissoring or styling.

Some features to look for are hydraulic tubs and raised tubs with ramps to reduce back strain caused by lifting heavy, larger breeds and bending over low tubs. Tubs that are open on three sides enable the groomer to reach both sides of a large-breed dog without the strain of turning the dog around or reaching over the animal.

Your shop will require standing dryers, velocity dryers and cage dryers. Warm-air drying units, which provide controlled warm-air flow from all sides, drastically reduce drying time (in most cases to 10 to 15 minutes).

OWNER'S NAME: *Smith, Mary*   PHONE: *555-1234*

OWNERS ADDRESS: *1234 Mayberry Lane*

Anytown, USA

PET'S NAME: *Shiloh*   BREED: *Keeshond*

NOTES: *Requires longer drying time—otherwise, well-behaved. Shiloh dislikes having her paws worked-on.*

AVERAGE FEE: *$35.00*   DATE FIRST GROOMED: *3-12-99*

HISTORY: *Bathed, brushed-out, nails cut 3-12-99*

Bathed, brushed-out 4-25-99

Flea bath 5-10-99

Bathed, coat-conditioner, combed-out, nails cut 6-14-99

Flea bath 7-11-99

Keeping a file on the animals you have groomed will help with scheduling, as will reminder cards.

GROOMING APPOINTMENTS						
	MONDAY	**TUESDAY**	**WEDNESDAY**	**THURSDAY**	**FRIDAY**	
8:00	Chadwick "Fifi" Poodle		Michaels "Buddy" Cocker	Bentley "Stryller" Afghan		8:00
8:30		Jacobs "Pearl" Pug				8:30
9:00						9:00
9:30	Billberg "Kandy" Maltese				Legare "Ginger" Shepherd	9:30
10:00		Gibbons "Corky" Keeshond	Douglas "Kosmo" Pug			10:00
10:30				Dugan "Penelope" Poodle		10:30
11:00	Paquin "Goldie" Mix	Crawford "Rosie" Dachshund			Arnold "Moses" Clumber	11:00
11:30						11:30
12:00			Cullen "Dixie" English Cocker			12:00
12:30	Carr "Bear-Bear" Cocker	Buckley "Barney" Golden			Smith "Gretchen" Bassett	12:30
1:00				Nowicki "Misty" Cocker		1:00
1:30						1:30
2:00			Glennigan "Captain" Dalmatian		Campbell "Doctor" Shepherd	2:00
2:30	Morrison "Squirrel" Airedale					2:30
3:00		Carter "Digsby" Lab		George "Sophie" Cocker		3:00
3:30						3:30
4:00					Quinn "Mickey" Mix	4:00
4:30						4:30

The appointment book allows the groomer to see the schedule quickly.

Dryers should be safely installed with adequate electrical allowance. Most grooming shops require a 220-volt circuit to ensure an adequate electrical supply. Electrical usage in your shop will be high, considering the tools, clippers, dryers, lighting fixtures, and ventilation and air control units that will be in use.

Flooring should include comfortable mats to reduce the groomers' foot fatigue. Your flooring should be resistant to water and have a high drying and evaporation rate. Non-skid absorbent tiles are a popular choice for your bathing area.

Grooming tables should be adjustable to reduce the groomers' back and muscle strain. Tables should have a grooming noose and be placed in an open area that allows the groomer to stand on all sides of the table. All grooming supplies should be easily accessible.

Your reception area should be warm and inviting. Popular colors for this area are combinations of peach and aqua blue, blue and green, yellow and red, orange and hot pink, magenta and teal blue, and hunter green and white. Half-doors will allow you to look into the back grooming area, yet deter or prevent an "escape" of a dog from a groomer (and don't think it won't happen!).

Warm-air drying units are a great improvement over the clothesline method!

When designing a grooming shop, consider practical features, such as a variety of tubs into which animals of every size and breed can fit comfortably.

If you possess patience, understanding and compassion for animals, you probably have what it takes to be an excellent groomer's assistant.

Groomer's Assistant

Most groomers are desperately in need of reliable assistants. Groomer's assistant is a career choice that doesn't require any special education or formal training and has no age boundaries. The only requirement is a love of animals! If you possess patience, understanding and compassion for animals, you probably have what it takes. This is an excellent career choice for any individual who might be thinking of a career in the grooming field. It will give you the chance to learn grooming techniques and grooming shop operation firsthand. The experience you gain as an assistant will be beneficial to your final decision about becoming a professional groomer. You may find that, without this hands-on experience, you would not have been able to make a correct career choice.

WHAT DOES IT INVOLVE?

The responsibilities involved may differ from one groomer to another. You will find that most groomers will require assistants to do pre-bath brushing, bathing, blow drying and perhaps *some* scissoring. Other duties might include washing towels, cleaning tubs, sweeping up hair, clipping nails, walking dogs, handling customers and scheduling appointments. Each groomer will have individual requirements for exactly what will be expected of you. Groomers may also vary regarding salary. Some may pay you a percentage of what the shop earns, while others may pay per animal or per hour.

FINDING EMPLOYMENT

When seeking employment as a groomer's assistant, you should prepare a resumé listing any experience you might have had working with or caring for animals. Formal education is usually of less importance than your real experience working with pets. List this experience even if this care is limited to your own pets.

You must also emphasize your desire to learn grooming as a trade. As with any resumé, you should include your employment history, length of time in each job, and reason for leaving. (There are many good books available at your local library that will enable you to write a job-winning resumé.) After completing your resumé, send a copy to every groomer and grooming shop in your area.

Follow up on your resumé with a phone call or personal visit. Do not be discouraged if the groomer is too busy to talk to you if you just show up or have not asked the groomer to suggest a convenient time. Instead, try to schedule a time to meet that is convenient for *both* of you. When you meet with the groomer, dress neatly and be polite; first impressions are lasting impressions. Be sincere when explaining your interest in learning the grooming business. Most groomers will be deeply influenced by your strong desire to learn the trade, and this factor will be very important in securing a job.

Self-Service Grooming Salon

The main concept behind the self-service grooming salon is convenience for the customer. Potential customers will utilize your service simply because it's so much easier and cleaner and less time-consuming than grooming their pets at home. Average pet owners do not have the proper equipment to bathe, brush out and blow dry their pet(s).

When the average pet owner does attempt to groom a pet at home, the results are backaches from leaning over a low tub; a dirty tub; a hair-clogged drain; and unattractive, water-splattered walls (dogs love to shake when wet!). After the bath, the pet owner is faced with drenched towels, wet floors and soiled carpets, as well as a wet dog under the bed. To dry the animal, the owner must be able to hold the animal down with one hand, brush with the other, and search for a third hand to hold the blow dryer (which was designed for human hair, not animals')! What a mess!

What a time-saving convenience for the pet owner to have a self-service grooming salon, or "do-it-yourself" pet-o-mat, in the area.

At the pet-o-mat, the customer will find a complete and private grooming station to rent. The customer will be delighted to find higher tubs with hoses, high-powered dryers and/or drying crates, grooming tables with restraining nooses, brushes, combs, de-matters, towels, non-slip floors, and NO MESS TO CLEAN UP!!!

EQUIPMENT

The following is a partial list of what you will need to get started. Go over the list carefully.

1. A shop, zoned properly, with appropriate licenses and permits. Your shop can be a converted basement to start with. Please remember to check local zoning laws pertaining to home-based businesses.

2. Insurance!

3. Separate grooming stations. Ideally, the animals should not be able to see each other!

4. Bathing tubs. These tubs should be set at waist level. Hydraulic tubs are nice, but expensive. Pet ramps work just as well, and can eventually be replaced as your business grows. You might also consider the benefits from having at least one

A self-service grooming salon offers the customer an alternative to drenched towels, wet floors and dirty carpets.

hydraulic tub station; you can rent this station for a slightly higher fee to recover any additional equipment expense.

5. Non-skid grooming tables. Your grooming tables should also be outfitted with a grooming arm and a grooming noose, to keep the dog steady and in an

upright position. This enables the pet owner to have both hands free for brushing and drying his or her pet.

6. "Tons" of highly absorbent towels. You should also have a washer and dryer on the premises, for convenient cleaning and sanitizing of the towels.

7. Numerous different grooming supplies, such as brushes, combs, clippers, shampoos, coat conditioners and flea dips. It is a smart business idea to have a small retail area at the front of your shop in which you might carry shampoos, coat conditioners and flea products.

   Brushes and combs should be provided, free of charge, at each grooming station.

8. Flooring suitable for comfort on feet and quick mop-ups. I suggest a flooring specifically designed for such purposes, one that is non-skid.

9. Cash register, display shelving and fixtures.

10. Sufficient lighting, heating and/or air conditioning.

11. Large water heater, sufficient plumbing system and electrical system.

12. Miscellaneous items, such as wastebaskets, aprons, brush and comb disinfectant, cleaning disinfectant (make sure that all cleaning solutions are non-toxic to animals), file cabinets and other office equipment.

Start-up costs will vary, averaging $1,000.00 per station. This figure is strictly as an estimate; the actual figure may be a little lower or higher, based on your location and other factors. Starting with a few stations, and eventually adding more as your business expands, may be the more practical and logical route. Remember, when designing your shop, to leave room for expansion, and always design your stations to allow for privacy and convenience.

You should have an attendant on duty at all times. In the beginning, this will probably be you. You may require additional help as your business grows.

STATION RENTALS

Clients will rent stations from you for a fee. Rentals can be by the animal or station, or by 30-minute intervals. Experience will enable you to decide which method or system will work best for you. This fee includes rental of one grooming station, which should be equipped with tub, dryer, grooming table, brushes, combs and towels. Clippers should incur an additional charge to cover your costs for upkeep on the blades. When setting your fees, you must keep in mind local groomers' usual fees. Your rental fee should be lower than a groomer's fee.

You have the option of assigning appointments or accepting walk-ins, depending on the size, locale and popularity of your business. Walk-ins will probably be suitable in the beginning. Remember to request that all dogs be leashed and all cats crated.

As I have mentioned with regard to professional grooming shops generally, it would be a smart business idea to have a small retail area strategically placed at the front of your shop. You could sell such items as shampoos, conditioners, flea products and grooming supplies. Animal treats and dog cookies should prove to be big sellers! You might also include any kind of animal art, or animal-related hand-crafted items such as household items decorated with images of different breeds. Diversify with consignment sales, or rent shelf space to local artisans to display their handcrafted merchandise.

Remember to do the following:

- Always give customers and their pets personalized attention. Offer free plastic, vinyl or disposable aprons (imprinted with your logo, of course!) for the rental customer to use. Have soft drinks and/or coffee available for purchase. Relate well to the pets, and have treats on-hand for them.

- Always make sure all stations, including all grooming tools supplied, are completely cleaned, properly sanitized, and thoroughly disinfected for each client.

- Advertising is a must. The more you advertise, the more clients you will reach. Advertising will need to be very heavy in the beginning but should taper off to a minimum, with an ad to announce specials (good during flea season) and a yellow page listing.

- And always obtain legal advice before investing in any business venture.

Grooming Station Leasing

Another concept similar to the pet-o-mat (see the previous section) is that of the grooming station leasing shop. In this grooming operation, you will follow the same basic format as the pet-o-mat, only you will be leasing the stations on a more regular basis and *to professional groomers*.

Groomers will have a lease contract that entitles them to lease a station from you at an established rental fee for a predetermined period of time as set forth in the lease agreement. The groomers set their own charges and carry their own insurance. Essentially they are self-employed, independent contractors.

HOW DOES IT WORK?

The groomer pays you (the shop *owner*) a regular weekly or monthly rental fee. Along with this regular rent, the groomer might also pay an additional percentage of his or her weekly earnings.

The rental fee should cover the groomer's use of the shop, its equipment and towels, any advertising the shop does, and a private grooming station. The *groomer* should furnish any special tools he or she uses. You, the shop owner, should supply grooming tables, tubs, dryers, kenneling or cage banks, heat, water, light and grooming utensils. Soaps and clippers are items for which you may wish to share the costs, include the costs in the rental fee, or have the groomer supply them.

The groomer might decide on his or her own hours and may or may not be required to be on-duty a specific number of hours each day or "turn out" a specific number of groomings. All fees collected by the groomer are retained by the groomer, who need not disclose total amounts taken in unless rental agreements include an additional percentage fee. The groomer handles bookkeeping, accounting and taxes. Therefore, as mentioned, the individual groomer is not an employee of yours.

A six-month to one-year lease should be required, with a four-week notice of termination, or renewal.

YOUR JOB

This is a fantastic business for those who wish to be self-employed yet do not want to carry the burden of employees. Your job will be very basic: managing the shop, cleaning and maintaining equipment, providing supplies and handling promotional advertising. Your obligations and revenue source are comparable to those of a landlord.

Before you begin, you should do the following:

1. *Check* into liability insurance for your shop.
2. *Consult* an attorney.
3. *Consult* with a business analyst or accountant before determining your fees.
4. *Preplan* your business down to the smallest detail before attempting to operate a grooming station leasing shop.
5. *Enroll* in a business course at your local college.
6. *Learn* all you possibly can about grooming! You will need this information to design your grooming stations and to operate your shop successfully!

ATTRACTING GROOMERS

To obtain groomers, you can advertise for groomers in your local newspaper's "Help Wanted" ads. You should also advertise station rental in the "Business Opportunities" or "Business/Store Rental" sections of the same newspaper. Another possibility is to obtain a mailing list from local groomers' associations and to conduct a direct mailing to members of these associations.

When doing any kind of direct-mail marketing, you should remember that the *only* impression your prospective clients will receive of you and your business is your brochure or flyer. You should always strive to make a professional impact by using attractively designed letterhead on the best quality stationery you can afford.

CHAPTER

4

All-Breed Pet Care Services

What You Have to Offer

I f you have *many* years of experience in animal care, and if you know at least a little about a lot of different things, then an all-breed pet care service might be the business for you. This type of business provides assistance in many different areas of pet care, so you will need a general knowledge of each different service you are planning to offer. Most of the information is readily available to you at your local library, but you should already be quite experienced in many of the different services you will offer.

If you start a general pet care service, you may consider offering any or all of the following:

- Basic grooming and coat care
- Feeding/medicating (nutritional advice plus a feeding program specifically prepared for the individual pet)
- Cleaning/disinfecting kennels, runs, units, wall banks
- Professional and reliable pet-sitting service/24-hour emergency pet-sitting (see chapter 6)
- Airport pickup and delivery service
- Vet taxi
- Exercising and walking
- Kennel/cattery assistance
- Expert animal training on your premises
- Pet placement service
- Veterinary referral service
- Lost-pet recovery program
- Breeder referral

- Pet care info tapes and hot-line
- Temporary help for pet shops, veterinary clinics, kennels, groomers
- Pet paramedics

....

A sample ad for general pet care services might look something like this:

Here at PetCare, we care about your pet! We have a completely trained and knowledgeable staff that is eager to serve your pet's needs. Each one of our employees has the experience and qualifications to offer competent handling of your pet along with lots of TLC! Give us a call today!

PetCare
Route 3
Yourtown, USA
555-5657

BASIC GROOMING AND COAT CARE

Your grooming service should target clients who hire you to groom their pets on a biweekly basis. A biweekly grooming session should be nothing more than brushing out the animal's coat, bathing and blow drying the animal, cleaning ears and teeth, and clipping nails. You should not be involved in any type of professional styling such as clipping or scissoring unless, of course, you are a professional groomer and wish to offer professional grooming to your clients!

FEEDING, NUTRITIONAL PLANNING AND MEDICATING

Nutritional planning is easier than it seems. A well-balanced diet is essential for a healthy pet. Some pets require diets geared toward specifics such as obesity or other health problems. Other pets need diets specially prepared for their lifestyle; for instance, hunting dogs, working dogs, and coursing hounds all need diets specially formulated for their active lifestyles. Likewise, show dogs need diets that will promote a healthy coat and muscle tone. Some investigation and research will help you learn about the different nutritional needs required for each animal.

CLEANING/DISINFECTING KENNELS AND RUNS

You probably have basic knowledge regarding cleaning and disinfecting kennels. Disinfecting is an absolutely essential precaution for the control and prevention of disease. Remember to check the disinfectant you use. It must be determined safe and approved for use around animals.

AIRPORT SERVICES

Airport pickup and delivery shouldn't be difficult unless, of course, you live 200 miles from the nearest airport! Learn the regulations and specifications involved in shipping animals *before* you attempt to offer this service. Most airlines are happy to offer you this advice.

Remember these safety precautions if offering this service:

- Never, *never* leave a pet in the car while you run into the airport (or anywhere else, for that matter).

- Make sure that the animal you ship has plenty of water.

- Verify takeoff time with the airline (if the flight is to be delayed for a significant amount of time, ask to remove the animal from the "cargo hold" for the period of the delay).

- Immediately offer water to any animal that has just had a long flight.

- Notify the airline immediately if an animal appears to be ill after a flight.

VET TAXI

With this kind of service, you provide transportation to a boarding kennel, grooming shop or veterinarian. If you take an animal to a veterinary clinic, you stay there with it, then take it home. Payment for the animal's veterinary costs can be arranged beforehand with the veterinarian, or paid directly to you for payment at the clinic, or paid by you to the clinic and reimbursed by the client immediately upon your return.

EXERCISING AND WALKING

Almost as simple as it sounds. Offer your clients different regimens or plans for exercising their dogs. For instance, you might offer to take them for a run (on leash, of course!) on paths at your local park or in a forest preserve (great exercise for you, too!). Or how about a brisk walk through the back roads of your community? Charge the customer a flat hourly rate. Terrific fun for both you and the pets. It is also a business you can start at any age, with little or no money. If business booms, add some employees. These should be relatively easy to find because the hours are flexible and there are few requirements other than reliability.

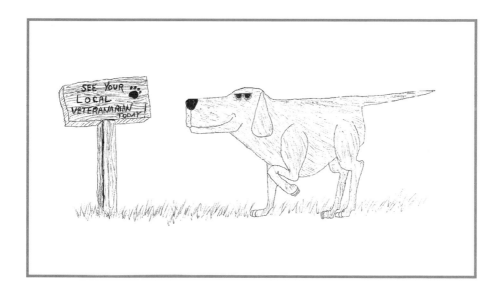

One service you can provide is a vet taxi for injured or ill animals.

KENNEL/CATTERY ASSISTANCE

You will assist with the general day-to-day operations of a kennel or cattery. Kennel or cattery owners might have a specific job in mind when hiring you or requesting your service, or they might need you to oversee the whole operation in their absence.

ANIMAL TRAINING

If you have a general knowledge of working with animals, you might offer this service. There are many good books available that will help you with specialized areas of training as you get beyond the nitty-gritty.

If you currently have a pet, you may wish to enroll in a local training session to familiarize yourself with the latest in animal training. If you don't have a pet, offer to take the neighbor's free of charge. The neighbor would probably welcome your offer.

Once you have considerable experience beyond the basics and have worked with numerous animals by assisting someone else (or perhaps several different people), you will be able to work with a client's pet (and him/her) on the client's own property. Here, there will be fewer distractions for the pet, making it easier to train. Work back and forth with *both* the pet and the client. Teach the client the proper method of training the dog, and work with the client and the dog to achieve a training method that works well for that individual animal. After all, that's what you're there for, to tailor the training regimen to each animal. You are a personal trainer.

ALL-BREED PET CARE SERVICES

PET PLACEMENT SERVICE

With this service, you try to locate good homes for pets. The owner of the pet will pay you a pre-established fee for this service. You might even consider compiling a list of "foster pet" homes, which might obtain funding through the owners of pets to be placed, or by a local charity, fund-raising drive, or donations from the public for a foster home program.

To place a pet, you might try advertising in the local paper with a picture of the "pet-of-the-week" and a brief description of the animal's qualities and traits. Thoroughly screen *all* prospective new owners and foster care providers. Some specifics to look for when placing a pet are the following: availability of a fenced yard, sufficient income to care for and feed the pet, and a general knowledge of proper pet care, as well as a household and lifestyle that fit the pet in question.

VETERINARY REFERRAL SERVICE

Here, you will obtain working knowledge of all your local veterinarians and veterinary clinics. Such a database should include how long the veterinarians have been in practice; what type of services they specialize in (such as eye care or dysplasia); whether they perform their own surgeries; whether they take emergencies; whether you need to set up an appointment (or whether they take walk-ins); and whether they are familiar with exotic or rare pets, birds, rabbits and so on.

This knowledge will help you refer the customer to the veterinarian who will best meet the customer's needs. You might charge the veterinary hospital a listing fee, or you might charge your client a search and referral fee.

Make sure you obtain proper insurance coverage! Can you imagine the consequences of referring a client to a veterinarian and then having that veterinarian make a mistake? Hopefully, this will never happen; however, you want to make sure that you are properly covered in the event that it does.

LOST-PET RECOVERY

With this service, you help locate lost pets. You may offer this service free, with a fee charged *only on recovery*, or you may wish to charge the customer a daily or weekly search fee.

When searching for a lost pet, you should look first at the neighbors' houses (take a photo along with you). Not surprisingly, many lost pets are recovered trapped in a neighbor's shed, garage or crawl space. (Cats *usually* do not wander more than a half-mile from their home.)

Your next step will be to post pictures of the pet around the general location of the lost pet's home or "last seen location." The best place to hang a "lost pet" poster is at the local school. Children are much more likely to spot a pet and remember it than are adults. Place these pictures where they will be easily noticed. Some high-visibility spots are grocery stores and service stations. Bright colors on your posters will make them more noticeable, as will the word "REWARD" written boldly across the top. If at all possible, get posters out within 24 hours of the time the animal was lost.

Additionally, check with the local police department, animal shelters, veterinarians, and both the county and local animal control office or animal warden.

Finally, you will want to place an ad in the paper. You might wish to discuss the possibility of your client offering a reward for information leading to the recovery of the lost pet.

BREEDER REFERRAL

In order to be able to give advice on different breeds, you will have to know the traits and care requirements for each and every one of the hundreds of different breeds! There are many books available that will give you excellent information on each breed, and other books that are not so good. The best information usually comes from the national club for each breed. Addresses for these clubs can be obtained from the American Kennel Club for dogs and the major cat registry federations for cats.

You should keep this information by the phone where it will be handy, and you should compile your own list. For instance, you could make lists of breeds that are good with children; that adapt well to apartment life; that are small, medium or large; that are easily trainable; that shed little; that are easy to care for; or that have strong guarding/ protective instincts.

Different people need different pets to fit their lifestyles. A "wrong pet" will only end up being neglected, rejected or, heaven forbid, brought to a shelter. The "right pet" will be properly cared for and loved by the right family. It's up to you to help decide which would be the right pet for each client.

Before you even recommend a pet to a client, make sure your client understands what is involved in *responsible pet ownership*. Explain to your client that owning a pet is a big decision that shouldn't be made hastily, or on the "spur of the moment." Stress that the pet will be with the client for life, and will require constant love and care. Make sure your clients are informed about the costs and responsibilities of owning pets. If you sense that a client may not make a good pet owner, work with that person a little more. You want to make sure that a client is fully capable of taking good care of an animal. If you have any doubts, suggest that he or she think about it for a few more weeks before making a decision. By delaying the decision, you often can deter a "bad prospect" from purchasing a pet. Most good prospects will still want to purchase a breed suitable for them.

You have to refer the right breed for each person. In a sense, you have become a "matchmaker." For instance, you wouldn't recommend a Saint Bernard to a retired woman living alone in a studio apartment, would you? The right choice for this person might possibly be an Abysinnian cat, which is easy to care for and will make a very loving companion. The same with someone who needs a dog that will be "okay" left alone while the owner works, maybe even guard the house while she/he's away, and can accompany the owner hiking on weekends. Would you recommend a Chihuahua to this person? Probably not! You would recommend a hardier, larger and probably more independent breed.

Once you have chosen the right kind of pet—and made sure that the prospective owner fully understands the responsibilities involved in pet ownership—you will then help locate that particular pet for him or her. This is where you use your "pet referral" service. When referring a customer to a breeder, make sure that the breeder you are recommending is knowledgeable and responsible and has a good reputation. The breeder must be a respectable and ethical person who breeds for quality, never for a product to sell, or for profit or quantity. Never refer a client to a "questionable" breeder. If you have any doubts at all about a breeder, visit the breeder's home, or kennel, and inspect animals directly. Ask questions regarding the way they care for their animals and how many litters they average (if they are producing many large litters, question that!). Ask the breeder whether they show their animals and whether they breed for proper temperament and the breed Standard. Remember, refer only the best breeders, and refer the "right" pet to the "right" person.

TEMPORARY EMPLOYEE SERVICE

Your professional clients might sometimes find themselves without the services of their employees. Employees get sick, take vacations, or even quit without notice. These business owners will need temporary help in a hurry. For instance, a busy veterinarian may need an assistant for the afternoon, or a groomer may have over-scheduled and may desperately need someone to fill in for the day to help with bathing. Or a pet shop owner may need sales-floor assistance two days next week. These businesses and others like them would benefit from a temporary employee service.

Your employees should be knowledgeable in the services offered. You should have sufficient experience to train your employees personally for positions in these fields.

PET PARAMEDIC

As a pet paramedic, you will be called to assist in emergencies—for example, pets that may have become trapped somewhere. You will have to be able to free animals from various situations and stabilize them for transportation to a veterinarian. You should be able to clean and bandage wounds, and splint broken bones. Your equipment should include a hard surface with adjustable restraints, gloves, towels, blankets, a stun gun and pet-carriers. You will also need assorted first-aid supplies such as antiseptics and disinfectant for cleansing wounds, along with bandages and splints. Additionally, you should carry miscellaneous equipment to free trapped pets; for instance, you should have easy access to a saw, chisels and grease.

Your fees for an emergency service could range about $65.00 for the visit, $30.00 for transportation to the veterinarian, plus additional costs such as disinfectant and bandages. In any case, your fees should be consistent with those charged in your area.

Ask your veterinarian for information and training in emergency situations, or contact local adult education sources.

Clients Mean Business

Getting clients means *reaching* clients. You can reach clients by making yourself visible wherever and whenever the opportunity presents itself. Send out flyers to groomers, private and boarding kennels and catteries, pet shops and veterinary clinics. Post your flyers at veterinary clinics, pet shops, grocery stores and Laundromats. Advertise in your local paper.

All-Breed Care

- Grooming
- Training
- Boarding

ABC All-Breed Care
1022 North Main Street
Any Junction, USA

Suzanne Meyers
Owner
(000) 555-5031

Sample Business Card

A business card like this one can expand your business by indicating the variety of services you offer.

Operating a Pet Care Service

When you first start out, you will more than likely be able to handle most of your clients yourself. As your business grows, however, you will find it necessary to hire crews or part-timers to help with the work.

Your fees, in this type of multiservice business, will vary according to each kind of service that you offer. Different services will require hourly, daily or flat-rate fees. For instance, the fees for pet-sitting may be per day; for airport

TODAY'S PET CARE SERVICES	Time	Estimated Time	EMPLOYEE SCHEDULED
1 Smith, grooming	8:00 a.m.	1 1/2hr	Belinda Meyers
2 Petie's Pet Store, temp	9:00 a.m.	9 hours	John Brewer
3 Hartman, pet-taxi to airport	10:00 a.m.	3 hours	Self
4 Thomas, pet-sitting	8:30 a.m.	1 hour	Self
5 Thomas, pet-sitting	4:30 p.m.	1 hour	Self
6 Jacobs, grooming	11:45 a.m.	1 1/2hr	Belinda Meyers
7 O'Brien, training	2:00 p.m.	2 hours	Self
8 Kiesgen Kennels, temp	10:00 a.m.	4 hours	Hiedi Newman
9 Prange, exercising dogs	3:15 p.m.	2 hours	Hiedi Newman
10 Fieldstoak, grooming	2:15 p.m.	2 hours	Belinda Meyers
11			
12			
13			
14			
15			
16			
17			
18			
19			
20			
21			
22			
23			
24			

Once you have regular customers, keeping a daily employee schedule sheet will be necessary. Note customer's name and service requested in left column and employee assigned in right.

delivery, flat; for disinfecting a kennel, per hour, plus a charge for materials.

You will need to keep very accurate reports and accounts. Taking a business course at your local college can help ensure proper management of your pet care service. As always, obtain legal advice, and make sure you have the proper insurance to cover your business.

Aquarium Maintenance and Leasing Service

Have you ever sat in a waiting room? I'm sure you have. I'm also sure that, out of boredom, you looked around at your surroundings. The interior design most likely consisted of neutral-color walls; an old watercolor print, probably of a lily (albeit in a glass frame); and a nondescript plant set back in the corner. Did you also notice the people? Some were probably thumbing through a magazine, anxiously checking their watches. Others, like you, were looking around the room or trying to calm fidgety children.

Now, take that same waiting room and add an attractive aquarium display. The people will be more relaxed, the children will be entertained, and time will pass much more quickly as you watch the fish in the tank. An aquarium is interesting and actually creates a tranquil effect.

GETTING STARTED

Aquarium leasing involves setting up display aquariums in lobbies or waiting rooms and maintaining these tanks.

A list of potential customers might include physicians, clinics, veterinarians, dentists, social workers, retirement homes, lawyers, banks, business offices, restaurants, hospitals, day care centers and schools. The list goes on and on. You can obtain a good prospective customer mailing list from your local yellow pages. Be sure to include all professionals and businesses that might have a lobby, waiting room, display hall or showroom.

Your best approach to prospective customers may include mailing a brochure, then making a visit. The brochure should be attractively packaged. The envelope should look professional and have your company name

Attractive aquariums have a calming effect in busy waiting rooms.

printed on it. The brochure should also be professional and attractive. Never, never send a handwritten flyer or copies of one made on a copy machine, nor should you use hand-addressed envelopes. You are dealing with professionals and should present yourself as such.

The brochure should briefly outline your service and should point out the benefits of leasing an aquarium for display. Explain in your brochure that aquariums are proven to have a soothing, tranquil effect. Relaxing patients, soothing busy clients, and entertaining fidgety children are your key selling points. Aquariums also enhance the interiors of waiting rooms, lobbies and offices. Your brochure should not list fees and terms; this is best done in person. The idea of the brochure is to sell the potential customer on the benefits of leasing an aquarium package from you.

After sending the brochure, follow up with a personal visit. Again, you must present an impression of professionalism—and success! Dress accordingly in neat, clean suits; carry your pamphlets, pictures and contracts in an attractive attaché case. Be sure to set up and photograph several displays for just this purpose, and remember to include them in your presentation. These displays should be of different tank setups, ranging from the common to the more exotic and unusual. Use your imagination here, for these pictures will be a major selling factor.

Always leave a business card, or attach one to the tanks you service. A picture of a tank setup as the business card is a unique idea and a good advertising tool!

EMPLOYEES

All employees should conduct themselves as professionals at all times. They should be knowledgeable and communicate well with people and should always be dressed neatly, perhaps in a company uniform. These people should be willing to work odd hours because many businesses will request that aquarium maintenance be done before or after regular business hours. This will create unusual and irregular working hours for you or your employees.

Tank setups can range from the common to the exotic and unusual.

EQUIPMENT

The following is a list of aquarium maintenance equipment. You will find it necessary to carry this equipment with you. Keeping a file on each client will enable you to bring the proper equipment on each individual client visit. You will probably add your own supplies to the list as your business expands.

- Activated carbon
- Air control kits
- Airline check valves
- Air pumps
- Airstones
- Algae removers
- Ammonia testing kit
- Aquarium orna-
  ments/decorations
- Aquarium salt
- Dechlorinator
- Diaphragms
  (assorted)
- Filter brushes
- Filter cartridges
- Filter floss
- Fish bags and food
- Heaters
- Holding tank (prefer-
  ably 15-gal. size)
- Insulated transporta-
  tion boxes for fish
- Medications and
  tubing
- Net disinfectant
- Nets, assorted sizes
- Nitrate test kit and
  scrubbers
- Pails and buckets
- pH buffers and test
  kit
- Plants (plastic),
  assorted sizes
- Plastic containers
  (for wet supplies)
- Power filters
- Screwdrivers/repair
  tools
- Siphons (short to
  extra long)
- Suction cup for
  heaters
- Tool or tackle box for
  miscellaneous parts

Following is a list of what you will need for each tank package that you will set up. You may wish to add your own supplies for special tank setups, or different tank designs.

Tank Package for 30-Gallon Tank:

- Glass tank and cabinet stand
- Full hood and bulb
- 150-watt heater and thermometer
- Air pump
- Forty pounds of gravel
- Undergravel filter
- Outside power filter
- Airline tubing
- Plants (plastic), centerpieces or rock ornaments
- Fish (may be chosen according to the client's wishes)

· ·

Tank Package for 55-Gallon Tank:

- Glass tank and cabinet stand
- Full hood and bulb
- Twenty-watt heater and thermometer
- Sixty-five pounds of gravel
- Undergravel filter
- Outside power filter
- Air pump

- Airline tubing
- Assorted plastic plants and centerpieces
- Fish (may be chosen according to the client's wishes)

CONTRACTS

As in any leasing service, a contract should be made. This contract is for the benefit of both you and your customers. All contracts should contain the following:

- Length of term
- Costs to the customer
- Payment (due you) schedule
- Responsibility of each party
- Specifications of services

When creating contracts, please consult your attorney. Many questions may arise. For instance, if a child pulls a tank down (heaven forbid), who is liable for damages: your client; the lobby where the accident happened; or you, the leasing company?

BILLING

This should be done monthly, with a mailed statement. Your charges will be for two specific services: the leasing of the tank and your maintenance of the tank. For instance, in a one-year lease, your fee for leasing a 30- to 55-gallon tank may average $30.00–$50.00 a month. The fee for maintenance and service on that tank might average $18.00–$40.00 per month; this will depend on the going rates in your area. For bookkeeping purposes, you might consider two separate bills, with a total of $48.00–$90.00 due to you.

If a client requests maintenance only, it is usually done on either a monthly or bimonthly basis. The client is responsible for all equipment needed and should be billed accordingly. The client usually purchases a tank and employs you only to service it. This type of arrangement works best when billed by the hour.

General guidelines to follow are these:

- Prepare many different aquarium packages for your client to choose from.

- Arrange attractive fish communities. Often, the unusual can be more appealing. For some ideas on making fish stand out more, see the notes on aquarium backdrop colors in chapter 2, on pet supply shops.

- Conduct yourself as a professional.

6

Pet-Sitting

n-home pet-sitting is fast becoming a very popular alternative to boarding. Among the many benefits are these:

- The pet stays at home in safe and familiar surroundings.

- The pet is not exposed to disease or parasite infection sometimes associated with facilities housing many animals.

- There is the added advantage of giving the home a lived-in look during the owners' absence.

- In multi-pet households, it can be less expensive to hire a pet-sitter than to pay boarding costs.

··

EQUIPMENT

Following is a list of supplies you will need to begin your pet-sitting service:

1. Calendar
2. Telephone
3. Reliable car
4. Flyers/brochures and business cards
5. Mailing list
6. Pet-sitting contracts/veterinary-service release forms
7. Local-area maps for planning service and travel routes

Pet-sitting has not yet become an alternative to baby-sitting, but is often preferable to boarding a pet.

GETTING STARTED

The most important thing you need to start is a good mailing list. This list should consist of dog, cat, bird and other small-animal owners and breeders in your area. You can obtain some addresses by looking in dog, cat, bird and other pet magazines, as they usually carry breeder ads. Local vets *may* be able to supply you with additional names from their office bulletin boards. Other good sources are local cat associations and dog clubs, which might allow you to have a membership list. Show breeders are an excellent place to start, as many show enthusiasts house an animal population that is too large to be boarded. Since these breeders travel to many different shows and therefore spend many weekends away from home, your service could be essential to them!

After compiling a good-sized mailing list, the next step is to have flyers or brochures printed and mailed to the people on the list. To make that all-important "first impression," your brochures should be professionally designed and printed. Secondly, an attractive, eye-catching business card should be posted at pet shops, grooming salons and veterinary clinics. Follow this by placing ads in your local paper.

FEES

When deciding on a fee, you should consider several factors:

1. *Travel distance*. Miles cost time, and gasoline costs money. Some clients may be as close as next door, while others may live 30 miles away.

2. *Number of pets to be cared for*. It is only logical that it will be less time-consuming to care for one pet rabbit than to clean and feed a kennel of 20 Great Danes.

3. *Number of visits required, per day, to the client's home.* This will be based on the kind of pet or the client's request.

4. *Other duties,* for instance, watering the garden, collecting the mail, or coming by at various hours just to "check up," if you have contractually agreed to any or all of these services.

Most pet-sitting fees range between $5.00 and $15.00 per visit, for the average pet owner, but fees depend upon the geographic area. The average charge is $10.00 for one-half hour to $15.00 for one hour, per pet. A charge for each additional cat and dog, per visit, is also customary in most areas.

PET-SITTING SPECIFICS

Your duties as a pet-sitter will consist of feeding, watering, changing litter trays and/or bedding, cleaning kennel runs, light grooming, medicating (if necessary), playtime and walking and/or exercising the pet.

Other duties may consist of watering plants; collecting mail; adjusting the heat, air conditioning or lights; and taking messages. These duties should be decided on prior to the client's departure. Also, prior to the client's absence, you should become familiar with his or her house and get introduced (yes, introduced!) to all the pets you will be responsible for.

Pet-sitting duties include feeding, light grooming, walking and exercising the pet, and playtime!

Following are other precautions you should take:

1. Always make sure you have a signed permission slip allowing you to seek a veterinarian's services in an emergency, or if you feel that a situation warrants such action. This agreement should also state that the pet owner is responsible for all veterinary bills incurred. These medical expenses should be either paid directly to the attending vet or reimbursed to you. Be sure that you get the name, telephone number and address of the animal's regular veterinarian, and ask your client to notify the vet that you will be taking full responsibility for the pet in the owner's absence.

2. Have the client give you names and telephone numbers of people you could contact in an emergency. Also ask how you can get in touch with the client.

3. Make sure your client understands who provides the pet food. This must be worked out between you and the client, but is something the client usually provides. Clients should leave the pet food in their home, and it should last for the duration of their absence. Ask your clients to add a few extra days' supply, as an added safety measure, in case of a delay in their return.

4. Please make a note of how much food each pet receives, along with the times and amounts of medication, vitamins, treats and so forth. Also make a note of any special cleaning and care instructions. Remember to write down *everything* so that there will be no guessing later!

5. Learn the daily routine of the pets you are caring for—for example, their *"outside time," play time, and feeding time*. If you are caring for many different clients, have to make many visits in one day, or have to spend a good deal of time at any one place, you must work out a time schedule that is well-organized and convenient. Also, routine is very important to animals. If its normal, everyday routine suddenly changes, the pet will become confused and uneasy. Such stress can even cause a dog or cat to become physically ill!

6. If it's not yours, don't touch it! Please remember to respect others' property and privacy.

7. Have your clients alert their neighbors to your presence. A well-meaning neighbor may mistake you for a burglar!

8. Make sure you obtain a key!!!

HINTS

A few words of caution! Most dogs are very protective of their homes. Until the pet knows you and comes to expect your visits, always enter the client's home slowly and with caution. If you feel the need to protect yourself, a security gate of hardwood slat or wire or plastic mesh (the kind used in doorways to restrain pets and small children) can be held in front of you or placed between the pet and you as you enter the home. This may prevent a small or medium-sized dog from harming you.

Animal Photography

Animal photography is fast becoming a popular career choice. Many breeders rely on professional photographs of their dogs or cats for advertising and other announcements. Most publications contain several pictures of pets, and many pet owners include pet portraits in their family albums. I suspect that the future will see pet photographers visiting veterinary offices and pet shops, much the same as we now have photographers at children's specialty stores.

DO YOU NEED A STUDIO?

Animal photographers usually photograph their subjects in one of four popular locations:

1. A professional studio (this can be a portion of your home to start)
2. Natural, outdoor settings
3. Cat or dog shows
4. The customer's home

In a professional studio, you will most likely have to deal with nervous animals. Pets can become very intimidated by bright lights and unfamiliar surroundings. Some pets will pick up on the scent of a previous animal, and still others will wish to "mark" their territory.

In-home studios work best in the beginning. You may set up a small area in your home away from all traffic and noise. No disturbances, please!!!

Outside settings also have the disadvantage of unplanned interruptions. It is hard to keep an animal's attention when

Some pets may be intimidated by bright lights and
unfamiliar surroundings, while others will rise to the
occasion.

there are leaves to be chased, neighbors' yards to be explored, and squirrels that need investigating.

Show sites are great!!! You can attract many customers as their pets are freshly groomed, readily available and proudly being displayed. You can contact the club sponsoring the show for booth information or details on how to be the "show photographer." In the beginning, it would be best for you to start out at "matches" (informal but club-sponsored practice events) or some of the small events, until you build your reputation as someone who captures the best of any pet on film.

You will find that the client's home works best for you. Animals are naturally more relaxed in their own home. Most animals will get to know you while you are unpacking your camera and setting up, and will be more apt to cooperate with you, yielding a much better shooting session and quality photographs.

EQUIPMENT

You will need the following:

1. Camera and equipment
2. Business cards and brochures
3. A separate area in your home for a studio (optional, of course)
4. Backdrops
5. Kitty teasers: feathered or tinsel-ended rods that can be found at cat shows
6. Squeaky toys to capture dogs' attention

7. Darkroom, or other area for developing your film

8. Record-keeping system

9. Patience!

10. More patience!

GETTING STARTED

The main objective when getting started is making your name known. Getting recognition is one of the biggest success factors and challenges in any business. So, get out there and get recognized!!!

You can start by setting up a booth at a dog or cat show. Advertising in pet publications may also help in getting your name out there. Do not hesitate to mail out brochures. You can obtain a good mailing list from pet publications, veterinarians, cat clubs, dog clubs and animal registries. Contact pet shops and ask about making an arrangement to do a "special appearance" on an upcoming weekend; and discuss sharing advertising costs to promote this event. Also, when seeking potential customers, do not overlook horses, birds, reptiles and other animals! They are pets, too!

Use your best pictures for advertising. Get them out there where your potential customers will see them. This could be an outside display-type advertising at your show booth, or an advertisement on brochures sent directly through the mail or even on your business card. Another surefire way of getting recognition is always to make sure your signature is on each and every photo you take. This is the best advertising of all!

Sitting ❖ Pretty

Pet Photography

Professional Photographs
In Studio & On Location

GORDON JACOBS
Photographer

(000) 555-4397

Sample Business Card

. . . .

A business card can help advertise your pet photography business.

Once you have gained the needed experience and have made a name for yourself, consider offering your professional services as well as your photos to publishers of magazines, newspapers and books; pet food factories; manufacturers of pet products and animal accessories; professional advertising agencies; and brochure design companies.

PHOTOGRAPHING ANIMALS—
THE SPECIFICS

There is an art to photographing animals. You cannot tell an animal to pose, smile for the camera, be alert and look cute! You will need a great deal of patience and numerous rolls of film to get that one perfect shot.

To highlight your subject, you must be very careful that no background distractions appear in your shot. These include house decorations, lamps, toys and even owners' hands. The backdrop should be taped to the background wall and over a chair or table. Make sure that you are photographing at eye level with the subject.

Backdrops can be any type of fabric and should be a solid color, not a print. All colors are acceptable. Rich velvety blues work well for most cats and especially well for orange- or red-coated pets! Neutral colors, such as cream and beige, work best for most dogs. Experiment with different colors on various breeds to see what works best for you. For instance, an ebony oriental cat could look terrific on an emerald green velvet backdrop, which would bring out its beautiful green eyes. But green eyes are also enhanced by purple, lilac and lavender backdrops. Work with a variety of colors and fabrics to see what is right for you and the animal you are photographing.

You can create amusing and candid shots with props. Baskets and feathers work well for kittens; balls work wonders with puppies. If the animal seems at ease, try placing a piece of the background fabric over the animal's head and catching a peek-a-boo shot as the animal looks out. Use kitty teasers and squeaky toys to capture and hold the attention of the subject. Food treats also work well.

Before you begin your session, make sure all eyes and ears are cleaned, and all coats groomed. Cameras will pick up the *smallest* things. Another problem you might encounter, especially with blue-eyed animals, is "red-eye," a result of the light from your flash reflecting in the animal's eyes. This can sometimes be avoided by having the animal not look directly at the camera lens. Natural lighting from an outdoor setting or light from a nearby window will help to eliminate red eyes.

You will find that with practice, patience and plenty of film, animal photography can be a fun-filled and rewarding career. Remember, however, the word "patience." You will probably have to take several different shots, with various poses, to come out with even a few good ones!

I strongly suggest taking some photography courses at your local adult school or college so that you can be the best at what you do! Good luck and happy shooting!

The Mail-Order Supply Business

How can you own your own business, work from home and still make money? Mail order! Mail order is a thriving business that almost anyone can do! You need no special education, very little start-up capital, and you can begin at any age!

All you need to do is decide on a product, or many products, and sell, sell, sell! What kind of product(s) is up to you. Unusual, unique or hard-to-find products work best. Use your imagination, and aim for a product that is uncommon, different or not readily available at stores. If you don't, you will be driven out by your competition before you even get started.

There are many pet-related products you could market. Better yet—invent one of your own! These product ideas might include miniature-sized chew bones for Chihuahuas and other Toy dogs, Persian cat bibs, Afghan afghans, Great Dane feeders (large and raised), Cocker Spaniel snoods (for their ears) or bandanas, bird bells, cat hammocks, pet treat recipes, fashion jewelry (portraying different breeds), mini couches for cats, pet restraints, animal car seats, animal life jackets, and handmade crafts decorated with various breeds.

Some handcrafted items could include custom-made clothes for pets, pet beds and/or quilts, ceramics, wood carvings of different breeds, catnip toys, embroidered items, throw pillows, cross-stitch, paintings/artwork, nameplates, welcome signs, lawn signs, cat show "cage" curtains, appliquéd towels, placemats, and handmade appliance covers. Any pet-related item, whether for the pet or home or for personal use, will probably sell well.

Mail-order items can include beds or quilts for dogs, and any other pet products that are different and not readily available in stores.

GETTING STARTED

Once you have a product, or catalog of products, your next step will be to set a price for each product. When deciding on a price, you must consider your original cost, advertising, packaging and shipping, plus your profit.

A good rule to follow is the three-to-one formula. That is, if your product costs you $3.00, you sell it for $9.00. Higher-priced products usually do not sell well through mail order. If you feel you have to ask a high price for any product in order to clear a worthwhile profit, you would do best to drop that product and look for a different one to market.

ADVERTISING

After you have priced your product(s), your next step is to prepare for advertising. Many great pet publications are available, and most have very effective marketing or advertising sections.

Do not forget magazines that specialize in specific breeds, as well as general publications. Breed-specific magazines are an excellent place to advertise if the product you are marketing pertains to a specific breed—for example, Siamese "Jewel-of-the-Nile" beds or Dalmatian "fireman's hat" bowls.

There are other ways to market your product as well; one such way is direct-mail. To do this, you must obtain a good mailing list. Many pet publications have mailing lists available; you can also purchase a mailing list through a company that specializes in them. However you obtain your list, you will need an attractive brochure describing your product and telling customers why they need it! If you have several products, you might choose to have a catalog designed and sent to the people on your mailing list. Additionally, you may be able to list your product(s) through inclusion in another pet-related marketing catalog.

Mary Smith
222 Main Street
Anytown, USA 55555

F.F. Feline Fancies Ltd.,
2100 N. Center Street
Anytown, USA 55555

Dear F.F. Feline Fancies Ltd.,

Please find enclosed my order for more of your terrific cat products. I just had to send you this brief note to let you know how much my cat has enjoyed your wonderful products!

Thank you so much!

Sincerely,
Mary Smith

A successful mail-order product can generate repeat sales.

In mail-order advertising, a properly worded ad is *the* main ingredient for success. You must make your ad's very first sentence capture and grab the readers' attention until they get their checkbooks out and send you an order!

To encourage this reaction, try enclosing a return envelope with your direct-mail advertising. In magazine ads, you may wish to provide an additional bonus if an item is ordered before a certain date, or include an 800 number for credit card orders. A picture of your product can increase your sales, so add a picture whenever possible. A guarantee will also increase your response, and real customer "testimonials" will give validation to your product and assurance to the buyer.

It is equally important that your ad be *truthful* in describing the product. *Never* falsify a product's worth or capabilities, *never* promise something that cannot be delivered, and *always* offer a money-back guarantee.

REEVALUATION: YOUR PRODUCT—IS IT RIGHT FOR THE MARKET?

If you receive a very small number of orders, I advise that you reevaluate your product. Is it too expensive? Would *you* buy it? Is it a worthwhile product? Is there much competition? Is your ad eye-catching?

If your product is a good one and you feel the price is fair, then you must change your ad. Try a different wording or description, or change your opening line. Check out other successful ads, and see how they work on you. Keep changing the ad copy until you find one that works for you.

CAREER SUCCESS WITH PETS

If you feel that the problem is your product(s), drop the product! Spend some imaginative hours researching or thinking up a new product. Try different approaches to the same product to enhance its value or appearance. For instance, a simple feed dish might become a more marketable item if the pet's name were written on the side of the bowl or if it were decorated with a catchy saying like "Life is like a bowl of Chewies."

Keep trying . . . you will eventually hit the right product . . . It will then be time to sit back, put your feet up, and wait for the orders to come pouring in!!!

Pet Retirement Homes

Do *you* own pets? Odds are you do. Have you ever wondered what would happen to your pets if you were not able to take care of them? Sadly, the odds of your pet surviving losing you are very poor.

There are many people out there just like you. Most people become very attached and devoted to their pets, and many worry about what would happen if, for various reasons, they were no longer able to take care of their pets. Some people provide for them in their wills, but the sad truth is that many beloved pets are put down after the loss of their owner.

PROVIDING FOR PETS

The idea of a pet retirement home is unique and becoming more popular. A pet retirement home is a facility that cares for people's beloved pets in the event that the owners are unable to. It should be a home that provides love, comfort and shelter to these pets for the remainder of their years.

This provision can be made through reservation contracts. It is not an arrangement that should be handled through a will! Almost all wills mentioning pets list an animal as beneficiary of a trust; as direct beneficiary of an estate; or as a gift to a specific person, charity, or animal foundation, in exchange for the lifelong care of a pet. *Unfortunately, such provisions are not valid in most courts!* In fact, a trust may even be considered illegal! The reason is that the beneficiary of the trust is not human, but an animal, and animals have no legal right to enforce a trust. Making an animal the direct beneficiary is also not valid in most courts due to the complex rules of property law. Leaving a gift, or contribution, to a specific person or organization in exchange for a pet's continued care is also not valid. The courts can refuse to enforce "gifts on condition" wills.

So, how can owners provide you, the pet retirement home, with the funding for their pet's retirement? One possible way is for the client to pay you now. A contract can be drawn up by an attorney, and you can then put the funds into a separate account for the client, with prorated rebates annually.

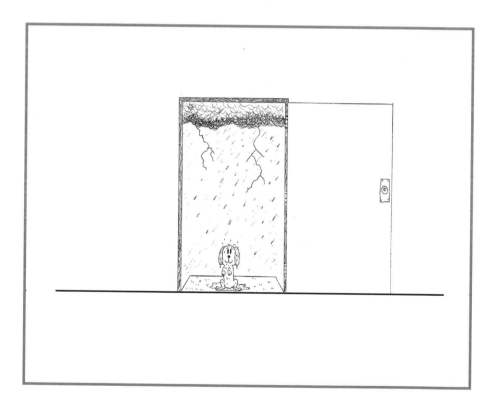

A pet retirement home provides comfort and shelter to pets when their owners are no longer able to do so.

PET RETIREMENT HOMES

The concept of a pet retirement home involves many complex details, and you will find the need to consult with a legal advisor on many matters. A drawback to the concept of a pet retirement home is that it requires a long-term commitment from you. You must be able to devote many, many years to the home. This is not a business you can start up and then change your mind and close your doors! It is therefore very important that you preplan your home down to the smallest detail.

A financial advisor is a must when figuring your start-up costs, operating expenses and fees (which will be discussed later in this chapter). The pet retirement home works for dogs, cats and other small pets, but can work as well even for horses, provided you have the space and have researched and preplanned every detail of the operation.

Remember to consider zoning and noise level regulations.

THE HOME ITSELF

A pet retirement home should consist of a house, building(s), and land of sufficient size to accommodate the cats/dogs comfortably. It should have at least one caretaker on duty at all times (yes, night shift, too). The number of employees must be in accordance with the number of pets being housed—usually one employee per 10 pets. The pets themselves should be offered all the comforts of home. Each pet should have a private or semi-private "suite" and be given large amounts of love, care and attention. Remember, all living creatures need love!

You could start this retirement home right in *your* home and, if business grew steadily, then move to a separate facility. Any prospective new site must be properly zoned and preferably as remote as possible from neighbors and busy streets. It should be securely fenced for safety and equipped with a security system and a caretaker. You might even include a pet cemetery on the premises. However, again, zoning is an important issue.

SETTING FEES

Clients will probably pay a one-time fee, yet certain circumstances may call for a monthly fee. This may be the case if a client has been hospitalized or physically unable to care for the pet.

There are many factors to consider when setting up a fee schedule. Mortgages, utilities, licenses, employees' salaries, insurance, feed, medications, legal fees, advertising and taxes are just some. The amount charged must be sufficient to cover your operating costs and should reflect the number of pets you house. The fewer pets you have, the more you will have to charge per pet. However, this type of sliding scale should be fixed in advance, as the fees cannot vary on a day-to-day basis. If they do, clients may feel that this is a less-than-honest operation. If you have so few pets that you are fully able to care for them all in your home, you obviously will be able to charge less than if you had the overhead costs of a separate facility.

Your fees should also reflect the age of each pet. For instance, the fee for the lifetime care of a pet must be suitable in each case, whether the pet is a 19-year-old Toy Poodle or a six-month-old Siamese kitten. Will the amount quoted cover the pet's food, shelter and health care—for another 17 or more years? You must know the answers before you begin.

GETTING FUNDING

An avenue for financial support might be found in charitable funding or donations. A third source is contributors' continuing support. Contributors benefit from your ongoing networking, advertising and promoting of *their* businesses. By becoming a supporting contributor, they are dramatically increasing their visibility and validating their company's ethical standing and position in the community.

Many different legal issues are involved in this type of business. Consult an an attorney, and thoroughly investigate every aspect before making even one commitment. Additionally, you should consider using an accountant when calculating your costs and profits. All contracts should include protection for you in case of "acts of God": fire, tornado, diseases, accidental death and so on. Contracts should also cover the action taken by you if the client, for whatever reason, stops payment.

Thoroughly investigate and preplan your pet retirement home. The pet retirement home is a lifelong commitment and should be treated as one. Are you prepared to love and care for these pets two, five, or even twenty years from now? Are you able to deal with the death of an animal that you have been caring for, and loving, all those years? If you have answered "yes," then this may be the right path for you.

CARING FOR THE SENIOR PET

As with any boarding facility, the home should be thoroughly cleaned and sanitized every day to maintain a healthy environment. All animals should be kept up-to-date on immunizations or inoculations, and have regular health checkups. Again, and above all, the pets should receive the love, care, time and attention they deserve.

The average life span for an indoor cat is almost 15 years. Many cats live into their early twenties; many dogs live into their mid-teens as well. As an animal ages, its needs change. An older animal requires a different diet, warmer quarters, better dental care and more frequent "accident" pickups. Signs and symptoms of old age include kidney ailments and disease, and kidney failure; thyroid problems; joint stiffness, arthritis and hip dysplasia; pigment changes, cataracts and other eye problems; tooth decay and gum disease; poor muscle tone; a dull coat and graying hair; brittle nails; and poor bathroom habits.

Older dogs, who are less active, require more fiber and a reduction in calories to help reduce or prevent obesity. Diets lower in protein are beneficial in reducing strain on older dogs' kidneys. Monthly or bimonthly veterinary checkups are recommended, as older pets are more prone to infection and disease; a mild infection in a senior pet can have serious consequences.

Older pets also require better dental care. You should *gradually* introduce dental care to a cat or dog who is not familiar with it. Begin by simply touching the animal's mouth area for several days to several weeks before. After the pet is accustomed to this, you should just wipe the teeth with a soft cloth the first few times, then *gradually* introduce the toothbrush. You can use a soft-bristled child's toothbrush, or you can ask your vet for a brush designed specifically for cats or dogs. Remember, when brushing an animal's teeth, *always* keep your fingers on the outside of the teeth!

An older pet needs extra affection; comfortable, calm surroundings; peace; some privacy from other animals; an

Older cats and dogs need warmth, gentle handling and tranquil surroundings.

adequate heating system; comfortable flooring and bed areas; and a familiar routine. Any change in routine will cause stress, which older animals do not handle well.

Older pets also need warmth, gentle handling, continued observation and tranquil surroundings. The diet should be formulated for the senior pet and should be easy to chew and digest. Sudden changes in behavior may indicate a health problem and require more careful observation and a veterinarian's checkup.

NOTE

The concept of a pet retirement home involves many complex details, as I have previously stated. I truly believe, however, that pet retirement homes are long overdue. Far too many innocent animals are needlessly euthanized each year simply because their loving owners were no longer able to take care of them. Their only crime? You tell me.

10

The Pet Referral Service

The pet referral service is one that locates a reputable breeder of a specific dog or cat breed for prospective buyers. Interested parties will contact a referral service for various reasons. Sometimes people are unable to locate the particular breed they are looking for. Or perhaps they don't have the time to search for the breed they wish to purchase or to screen each breeder individually. Often, potential pet owners are just plain unsure of which breed will best suit their particular lifestyle. Obviously, you must be very familar with and know the advantages and disadvantages of most breeds, for you will be making recommendations to these people. If you make a wrong "match," both the customer and the animal you recommended will be unhappy and unduly stressed, or worse!

GETTING STARTED

You will require very little equipment to start this business, and you can run it from your home. You will need a phone (with a separate number from your household's); a desk; an adequate filing system, which should be kept by the phone; brochures designed for the *breeder,* describing your service and how it benefits the breeder; brochures designed for the *buyer,* describing your service and how it benefits the buyer; and attractively designed business cards. A computer, along with a good database software program, is great if you have one; however, I do not feel this is absolutely necessary when you are just starting out.

You will also need forms for filing individual breed listings. These forms should include space for the breed, age, color and sex of the animal; the breeder's name, address and telephone number; and the date of the listing

(see the example). You may wish to have a separate section
(usually on the back) where you can list the names
and telephone numbers of people you have referred to a
breeder. This will enable you to follow up on referrals.
Always file these forms under the breed listed. This way,
when a customer calls seeking a specific breed, you will
have all files on that breed readily available.

It's important for a pet referral service to match
customers with pets that suit their lifestyles.

THE PET REFERRAL SERVICE

Before you begin your business, you will need a list of breeders to refer your buyers to. You can obtain a good list from several sources:

- Groomers
- Pet supply shops
- Veterinarians (look for bulletin boards with a client business card section)
- Dog and cat clubs or associations. Ask them for a membership list, or mail your brochures to the clubs themselves if they will not release a list of members. Many dog and cat publications have a classified section where you might find additional names and addresses.
- Dog and cat shows. This is an excellent way to locate breeders. Purchase a show catalog (which lists the exhibitors' names and addresses), visit with the exhibitors, and exchange business cards. Additionally, you can contact breeders by telephone and briefly explain your service to them; offer to send them some literature on your service, which they may look over at their convenience.

....

After you have obtained this good-sized list of breeders, you should have an attractive brochure printed. It is often possible to design this yourself. This brochure should explain your service and emphasize the benefits to both the breeder and buyer. People really do not care about how your service works; they want to know how *they* are going to benefit from it! Send every breeder on your list a brochure, a personal invitation to join, and a listing sheet.

Be sure to include a statement explaining to the breeder that all applications are accepted or declined at *your* option. You do not want to be obligated to refer a less-than-excellent breeder!

Keep track of the breeders who have received information packets, and follow up with a phone call if you receive no response. Printing and mailing costs will be your single biggest expense when starting your referral service. The next biggest expense will be your advertising and marketing campaign.

Cocker Spaniel

Breeder			Phone Number	
Address			Listing Date	
Sex	Color	Whelped	Price	Comments

Breed listing sheets help organize essential information.

ADVERTISING AND MARKETING

You must advertise, advertise, *advertise!* You should post notices about your service in pet shops, veterinary clinics, groomers and any other service that caters to pets and their owners. Every newspaper in the area you will service should carry a crisp, eye-catching, professional ad. Your ad should capture the customers' attention and "program" them to call you when they want to purchase a pet.

One method of doing this is known as the "fear tactic" (what will happen to customers if they don't call you). In your case, the customer risks purchasing a substandard or poor-quality pet, one that may be unhealthy or have a bad temperament. Subtly state that this could be the result of contacting a breeder which your service does not endorse as a preferred, recommended, quality breeder.

Another method of advertising is the "how can the customer turn down all these freebies?" In this method, you tell the customers just how much they will benefit from your service! For instance, you offer:

- Free referrals to qualified, pre-screened breeders who have proven to be ethical, and successful in producing quality animals and proud of it. These are people who breed because they are serious hobbyists, not because they are motivated by a source of income.

- Free, ongoing support in answering your customers' questions on pet care; "free, convenient, over-the-phone, perfect-matching" expert advice on selecting the right pet

- Guaranteed assurance that the recommended breeders are caring, knowledgeable people who meet your service's strict requirements.

- Assurance to the customers that they are under no obligation to purchase anything!

••

Your ad should be placed under the "Pets for Sale" classified section of all the newspapers with a circulation in the areas you wish to serve. You might want to start by just covering a small area, and then expand as your business gains in popularity.

The marketing method you use to gain the breeders' "membership" should put emphasis on the benefits breeders will gain from your service:

- Increased exposure
- Better, more reliable, pre-screened customers
- An enhanced reputation
- Visibility and integrity growth
- "Quality breeder" recommendations and endorsements

••

Your service will also showcase the truly good, caring breeders, as well as slow down and possibly eliminate bad breeders (whose only concern is not the quality but the quantity of animals they breed)—at least from your area.

If you are ambitious enough, you can work out a deal with local feed suppliers, veterinary clinics, groomers and pet shops to support your pet referral service by offering discounts to "members" of your service on the products or services they offer. This helps the pet-related businesses because you are networking their goods and services, and recommending many new customers to them. It gives you the added benefit of offering your breeders "membership discounts" on feed and other goods, through these cooperating merchants.

REFERRAL SERVICE FEES

There are two different methods of income from a pet referral service. You will have to do some experimenting to find out which is best for you. Or you may decide on a combination of both methods.

With the first method, you charge the breeder a listing fee. This fee can be based on different systems. You might charge a fee per pet sold or per litter listed, or a set, one-time annual fee for continuous referral during a period of one year. Since you might sell many pets for a given breeder, he or she will simply look at this fee as a form of advertising. Many breeders (but not all) will include this additional advertising expense in the purchase price of their pets. There are three different ways of collecting your fee with this method:

1. Your fee may be a commission based on a percentage of each sale. For instance, if your referral results in a $200.00 sale and your charge is a 10-percent referral fee, you earn a $20.00 commission.

2. Your fee may be based on listings alone—for example, a fee of $30.00 per litter listed or a fee of $20.00 per pet listed. With this method, you receive a fee regardless of the number or cost of the animals sold.

3. You earn an annual membership fee. The breeder pays you a fee that covers continuous referrals for a period of one year.

With Method 1, you will be working on a commission-*only* basis. This is how you make your money! With this method, it is very important that the buyer knows this. The buyer should be told to mention your referral to breeders and, in turn, inform you of any resulting sale. If in doubt, always follow up with a telephone call to both the buyer and breeder. Personally, I do not recommend this method as it is too time-consuming: You must follow up every single referral you make with calls to both the buyers and breeders.

Another method is to charge the *buyer* instead of the breeder for your referral. For example, you may charge the buyer to locate a certain breed of dog or cat of a specific color or sex. Your fee may differ according to the breed you are asked to locate. This is like a search or finder's fee that prospective buyers pay before any referrals are given to them. You may also offer a money-back guarantee if you are unable to locate the breed the buyers are looking for.

I would like to emphasize here that your *only* involvement in the sale of these pets is the *referral*. All agreements and contracts should be between the buyer and the breeder. At no time, and never, in any way, should you directly handle any animals! Do not offer to pick up or deliver a pet; nor should you handle breeders' contracts or health guarantees. Do not discuss purchase prices or the quality of any particular pet you refer to the buyer. Your *only* job is to locate the breeder of a pet the buyer is seeking, and *nothing more*.

No matter which method you use, remember that you should *never*, and I mean never, give out the breeder's address! You need only give the breeder's name and telephone number. Allow the breeders to talk to the prospective buyer and make their own decisions—that is, whether the prospective buyer would be a responsible pet owner and whether the breeder might be interested in selling a pet to this person. If the answer to both of these questions is "yes," the individual breeders may then choose to give this person their address.

OPERATING YOUR REFERRAL SERVICE

This business is relatively easy to operate, and enjoyable as well. You will not handle any animals or deal with any sales. Additionally, you will be helping put unethical breeders out of business, as you will only endorse "quality breeder" members.

This business has the added advantage of allowing you to work from your own home. You do not need any baby-sitters, you will not have to fight traffic, your overhead is minimal, you can work your own hours, and you can wear your housecoat! All you will need is a small area, just large enough for a phone and a filing system (no background noise, please).

You might consider installing an answering machine or obtaining "voice mail." You will also need an adequate bookkeeping system. If your business becomes too advanced for your filing system, you should consider installing a computer. A computer will help simplify your need to keep and search through the many files you will have on the many breeds you list. You should also have some breed books handy to help answer the questions on each breed you may be referring to a prospective pet owner. Just feed the names of the breeders, their phone numbers, pertinent information (such as years they have been breeding), and breed information into a large enough database system. Then, when a customer calls requesting a certain breed, you just "ask" your computer for an instant report on that breed and your members who work with that breed. What could be easier?

A LITTLE ADVICE

Many states, including Massachusetts, New Jersey, Virginia, New York, Michigan, Pennsylvania, California, and Florida, have laws governing the sale of cats and dogs. Check your state's laws and verify that the breeders you list comply with these laws.

I would like to pass on this bit of advice. KEEP YOUR BUSINESS CLEAN! This means: Do not refer clients to bad breeders! If you have had a complaint on a certain breeder, investigate that breeder thoroughly and do not use that breeder again if the complaint was justified. Always ask your buyers to let you know whether they were satisfied with the referrals you gave them. When in doubt about any breeder, it is best just to take that breeder off your membership list. You might consider starting an "ethical" breeders association, for which every potential member is thoroughly investigated and must meet certain require-ments and restrictions in order to become a member. This will give you better clout in your business, and better peace-of-mind in general. If you do use bad breeders, or continue to refer clients to a breeder about whom you have received numerous complaints, you are destroying your business's reliability and integrity. More importantly, you are being unfair to the buyers, and you are keeping bad breeders in business.

Operating a Career School

Because of today's rapidly expanding pet population, the interest in pet care is growing at a fast pace. This has created a need for better education and training in pet care and other animal-related careers. Many schools existing today are fine examples of success. Students sometimes pay thousands of dollars in tuition for an education in fields such as grooming and Obedience Training.

Operating a school specializing in pet career education could be a very profitable business. Many students wishing to learn a new trade, or expand on an existing one, would consider such an education a wise investment.

However, opening this type of school might require a large investment. You would need a building of suitable size to hold a classroom, a hands-on instruction room, or an actual "real life" working area, as well as restrooms; and enough land to handle any outdoor instruction, such as Obedience Training. You would also have to hire instructors, carry insurance, and pay for promotional advertising. If limited funding is a factor, you should start small and expand as your profits grow. This is the easiest and most practical way to cut down on initial investment costs.

Career Path Programs

There are many different courses of study your school might offer. Following are seven different popular career choices (you might even wish to add some of your own):

1. Veterinary assistant

2. Groomer

3. Dog trainer

4. Pet supply shop owner/manager

5. Aviary owner/operator

6. Boarding kennel owner/manager

7. All-breed pet care provider

VETERINARY ASSISTANT

In this program, a student will learn skills in the following:

Basic office work: Filing, billing, answering phones, scheduling appointments, record keeping, customer relations.

Aspects of animal health: The anatomy of animals, understanding and recognizing signs and symptoms, handling sick or injured animals, diseases, behavior problems and behavior patterns, learning what to do in emergencies.

Assisting in surgery: Veterinary terms, surgical instruments, operating room procedure, bandaging wounds, disinfectants and sanitation, caring for recovering pets, medications and how to dispense them, recognizing signs of complications and how to handle them.

General instruction: Breeding, emergency whelping, caring for the newborn, care for adult or senior pets, dentistry, proper sanitary measures, disease prevention.

GROOMER

Grooming courses should teach students the following:

Basic grooming procedures: Shampooing, bathing, combing and brushing out, de-matting, drying, clipping nails, ear care and dental care.

Many breeds, like the German Shepherd Dog, can be trained to be guard dogs or to work with the blind, deaf or physically challenged.

Clipping and styling: Learning how to groom different breeds of dogs and cats, and learning each breed Standard.

External parasite control: Recognizing and identifying the different parasites; learning about the chemicals used in flea products, and using flea products safely.

Hands-on grooming: Working with animals; actual experience grooming live animals.

Grooming tools: Learning about the different types of scissors, combs, brushes, mat splitters and clippers, and what each instrument is used for.

Operating a grooming business: Bookkeeping, record keeping, designing and equipping a shop, customer relations, advertising and marketing, employee management, daily operation.

DOG TRAINER

In this program of study, a student learns the essentials and basic fundamentals of training dogs for Obedience, guard work, conformation, and possibly for work with the blind, deaf, or physically challenged. Knowledge of animal behavior and various breed particulars is essential.

PET SUPPLY SHOP OWNER/MANAGER

In the pet supply shop owner/manager course of study, a student learns invaluable information on running a small business, such as the following:

Small-business management: Bookkeeping, accounting, estimating profits, profit and loss statements, marketing, advertising, inventory, loss control, ordering merchandise and merchandise stocking, working with brokers and pet-product representatives, daily operating procedures.

Store "make-up": Displays, endcaps, design, alarm systems, inventory, stock and seasonal items, cash register and check-out area, sales area, interior appearance, window displays, designing a layout plan for loss prevention.

Livestock: Recognizing the breeds and species of birds, fish and herpetiles; caring for different breeds; having some knowledge of dog and cat breeds; recognizing and handling parasites and disease; environmental control.

Customer relations: Developing good customer relationships, dealing with the difficult client, securing sales, establishing repeat customers.

Employees: Training, supervision, reading and verifying job applications and reference checks, absenteeism, payroll, insurance and other employee benefits, improving employee efficiency, writing an employee handbook and manual.

Pre-opening planning: Financing, insurance, business planning, market plans, zoning, location, store size, purchasing fixtures and display shelving, obtaining licenses, taxes, utilities, contracting.

AVIARY OWNER/OPERATOR

In this course of instruction, the student learns about bird genetics, sexing, breeding, offspring, nesting, caging, natural environment, temperature control and the individual characteristics and requirements of different species. The course should also include diet and nutrition, external parasites and their control, diseases of birds and species cycles. Additionally, the students should learn the fundamentals of owning and operating a breeding aviary.

BOARDING KENNEL OWNER/MANAGER

Here the student should have "hands-on" learning in an actual boarding facility as a sizable part of his or her learning experience. As an added bonus, the boarding kennel could generate additional income for your school through greater exposure of your programs to the public. The kennel could also pay a kind of "agency fee" to the school for sending a constant supply of willing workers. This fee could be the balance between a "learning wage" paid to the worker, and a regular employee's hourly rate. Topics to cover are these:

- Owning and operating a boarding establishment
- Building, layout, planning and kennel design
- Economics of successful kennel management
- Responsible care for pets
- Handling emergencies
- Handling behavior problems in dogs and cats
- Basic grooming, health and nutrition
- Sanitary measures to prevent the spread of disease
- Security and safety precautions
- Fencing, bedding and housing

ALL-BREED PET CARE PROVIDER

In this course, the student is taught all aspects of animal care, as well as the business of owning an all-breed pet care service. Some courses to include in this area of study are the following:

- Basic grooming and coat care
- Feeding and medicating
- Cleaning and disinfecting kennels, runs, caging units, wall banks, and all other animal facilities
- Training for in-home pet sitting
- Animal nutrition, health tips and proper pet care
- Working in a kennel or cattery environment
- Basic animal training
- Working knowledge of all the different breeds
- Working in a pet supply shop, veterinary clinic, kennel or grooming shop
- Emergency pet care

Whatever the courses of study offered, instructors need not be professional educators. Your staff can be assembled from the ranks of those who have been successful in each of the various fields. Each person need not teach more than one course within a given program. This should make it easier for people to commit to a smaller amount of time, as well as providing expert advice in a specialized area. After all, what could be better than learning from those who have had career success with pets?

12

Dog Show Handling

Do you enjoy traveling? Do you have the ability to work well with animals? If so, then professional dog show handling might be a good career choice for you. A professional handler is someone who earns a living by housing and thoroughly conditioning, training and preparing a client's dog for show ring competition. He or she then actually brings the animal into the ring for competition and, hopefully, wins! A rewarding career as a professional handler can be achieved only with the knowledge and experience gained through many years of apprenticeship as an assistant with an already established, successful handler, or after a like number of years as a successful, skilled amateur. Remember, people will be hiring you for the skills, knowledge and ability that they don't have but *you* do!

Handler's Assistant

Starting out as an assistant to a professional handler will enable you to learn handling basics. Additionally, you will gain valuable experience that will be useful if you decide to pursue a career as a professional handler on your own. As an assistant to a professional handler, you will be expected to be available to travel to dog shows and do the work involved in preparing the dogs that are being campaigned, both at home in the kennel and at the show. Often, especially in the beginning, an assistant will remain behind to oversee the care of dogs not being campaigned.

YOUR DUTIES AS AN ASSISTANT

As an assistant to a professional handler, you will be expected to assist in keeping the dogs in top condition!

Starting out as an assistant to a professional handler will enable you to learn the basics about animal behavior as well as handling skills.

This will include overseeing special diets designed to maintain good health and proper coat condition; exercising the dogs, which is vital to enhance muscle tone and proper gait; and daily grooming and bathing essential to keep the coats in top show condition. You will also learn about different coat conditioners, grooming techniques, vitamins and food additives, and proper dental hygiene, all of which you will use when working with the dogs.

However, aside from the daily chores involved in maintaining healthy show dogs, you will spend a good share of your time cleaning and disinfecting cages, crates, dog runs and dishes used for feed and water. Any facility that houses animals must follow a strict regimen of cleaning and disinfecting.

Among your duties, too, will be preparing for upcoming shows. This will include special attention to the dogs that are entered, packing proper equipment, and, of course, seeing to the dogs while "on the road." Additionally, you might be expected to help with the driving. At the show, you will help with unloading the dogs and equipment, setting up in preparation for grooming, and seeing to the overall care and preparation of the dogs.

You can learn more about handling by attending conformation classes in your area (bring a dog!) and visiting dog shows. Additionally, many books and tapes are available that include information on conformation handling and dog shows.

WHERE TO FIND EMPLOYMENT

When seeking employment as a handler's assistant, you should prepare a resumé that focuses on all your animal-related work experience. It is an excellent idea to accentuate your desire to work as an assistant and learn professional handling. Experience is a definite plus, but if you lack experience, you may be able to arrange an apprenticeship program, which will compromise on your wages while you are learning. Many handlers will offer room and board in exchange for work.

You will need to obtain a good mailing list of handlers to whom you will send your resumé. To get this list, check with dog registries (AKC, UKC), breed magazines, and any publication dealing with the show dog. You may also obtain a mailing list from handlers' associations, or kennels that specialize in showing dogs.

Once you have obtained a good mailing list, send out an attractive and informative resumé to each person on your list. There are many books available at your local library that will help you prepare a winning resumé geared especially to your target audience.

Good luck and happy showing!

Professional Handler

Although this can be a very profitable career, establishing a career as a professional handler may be a difficult goal to reach. Many professional handlers started quite young, usually in Junior Showmanship, and spent many years exhibiting dogs before acquiring a name in the business.

If you have apprenticed as a handler's assistant for a good length of time, you are probably familiar with the work involved. Most likely, you feel you have a sufficient amount of experience showing dogs and are ready to strike out on your own. You should have experience showing your own dog to a championship, which will further develop your skills and give you some visibility in the show ring. You could also approach show fanciers with your experience and knowledge, or place an ad in a magazine that specializes in the breed you are most interested in showing.

WHY A HANDLER?

Many dog owners will send their dogs out to professional handlers to be campaigned on show circuits, mainly for the title of champion. Owning a champion enables the owner to gain more respect and better recognition of his or her kennel name. The owner may then be able to introduce this dog of proven quality into a suitable breeding program for the enhancement of that breed, and to use the title as a mark of quality as judged against others of the same breed.

Many owners or breeders of show dogs will hire professional dog handlers to do this campaigning for them. The professional handler has more show knowledge and therefore a better understanding of the fundamentals of dog shows, judging, and show conditioning of the dogs than the average or beginning exhibitor. The professional handler can usually "finish" a dog in a fraction of the time it would take the new or even average dog owner.

SHOW HANDLING SPECIFICS

Show handling involves a combination of skills and knowledge. You must have an in-depth knowledge of each breed you handle. You must know how to handle dogs moving on a show lead; how to "stack," or pose them properly; and how to minimize their faults and draw attention to their virtues, or assets. You have to have a deep and clear understanding of each dog you are showing, *not just of the breed in general*. Learning the character of the individual dog enables you to emphasize desirable ring behavior (the dog should display alertness, and a proper gait according to the specific breed's Standard), while deemphasizing undesirable traits (such as shyness) in the ring.

Handling also involves knowing judges' preferences in each breed. By knowing what qualities a judge looks for in a particular breed, you will be better able to select the right dog to show under that person. For instance, you would not show a dog that is not a good mover under a judge who puts a lot of emphasis on soundness.

Aside from handling in the ring, you will have to have knowledge of grooming. *Grooming specifics for each breed vary.* You will have to know the exact grooming procedures for each dog you plan to show. You will have to know when and when not to clip and about proper bathing techniques for all coat types, brushing, combing, powdering, nail clipping, dental care and ear care. Additionally, you must know which grooming techniques will maximize assets and minimize faults—for example, scissoring, or clipping a coat to lengthen a short neck or broaden a narrow front.

This also means that you will have to know the breed Standard for each dog you show, and be able to compare your dog to the Standard. You must be honest and knowledgeable enough to evaluate each dog's good and bad points.

Professional handling also requires traveling nearly all year round. Much of this travel will be to distant states, so you should have a very reliable vehicle. Most likely, you will need a van or other vehicle that can hold numerous crates,

When showing any breed, such as the Bulldog, the handler should know the breed Standard and be able to determine how his or her specimen measures up.

grooming equipment, feed supplies, water bowls, newspapers for "pickups," cleaners and disinfectants, towels, shampoos, blow dryers, portable exercise pens and, of course, your suitcases. Be aware that traveling can often result in poor motel accommodations, rushed meals, and the aggravation of packing and unpacking again and again.

As a handler, you must have a kennel of a sufficient size to house the dogs you will be showing. You will need an assistant to help you with the everyday care of these animals. You will also need another assistant or kennel help to look after the kennel and its occupants while you are on the road. As with any facility that houses animals, a very strict routine of cleaning and disinfecting must be followed to ensure the health of the animals under your care and supervision.

One Last Word

Although it may be a difficult career goal to reach, professional show handling can be a fun and rewarding career. Remember to gain as much showing experience as you can *before* you attempt to offer your services as a professional handler. Once you have "finished" a few clients' dogs, you will probably receive more requests for your services than you can "handle."

Good luck! I'll be looking for you in the ring!

Veterinary Technician/ Hospital Employee

Veterinarians work with a branch of medicine that centers on the care, control and prevention of animal diseases and illnesses. A veterinary assistant helps the veterinarian with all sorts of duties. As a veterinary technician/assistant, you may assist with surgery, perform basic office work, work with the clients, and care for the animals.

Not every veterinarian will require that assistants do all of the aforementioned tasks. A veterinarian may assign only a few of these tasks to you. Let's take a look at some of the duties that your job might involve.

IN THE OFFICE

You will answer the phones and schedule appointments. You will probably receive many calls each day regarding inquiries about immunizations, health and behavior concerns, and general information.

You should be somewhat knowledgeable regarding most pet questions, as you will be expected to handle most of these calls on your own. You will also be expected to take clients' payments on accounts and make adjustments to accounts accordingly. Additionally, as an assistant, you will have to do basic filing and retrieving of patient files.

WORKING WITH THE CLIENTS/OWNERS

Part of your job duties will include working closely with clients/owners. You should feel comfortable working with people, as you will be working with them for the better part

Veterinarians deal with the care, prevention, and control of animal diseases. All this responsibility requires the help of an assistant!

of your day. A warm, friendly, polite personality is a definite must! You will be expected to answer questions concerning animal care and to listen (with interest) to the clients' stories about their pets. You will show the owner and patient into the examining room, and, more than likely, you will be responsible for cleaning the examining room after each pet has been seen and before the next patient enters. You will be accepting payments and rescheduling appointments after each consultation or appointment is finished. You also will have to explain the proper care regimen to the owner for each case the doctor sees.

HOUSECLEANING

YES! Every career has its drawbacks! As an assistant, you will be expected to clean up waiting room "accidents"; prepare examining rooms for new patients; and clean and disinfect the walls, cages and other areas of the facility where animals might be kept. Additionally, you might be expected to thoroughly clean all floors at the end of each day before closing.

SURGICAL DUTIES

You will be relied upon to assist the veterinarian in surgery. This may include administering medicine prescribed by the doctor, transferring surgical instruments, preparing the operating room for surgery, carrying out the doctor's instructions during the procedure and sanitizing the operating room before and after surgery.

The duties of a veterinarian's assistant may include everything from surgical assistance to housecleaning.

TENDING TO THE ANIMALS

You will be expected to oversee the care of pets in the animal hospital or clinic. This includes feeding and medicating the animals, cleaning their cages, and observing them for signs of trouble during recovery. You will be expected to recognize any signs of danger and notify the doctor of any changes in an animal's condition or behavior. You will also be expected to keep a chart on each animal admitted to the hospital.

SEEKING EMPLOYMENT

If you are interested in a career as a veterinary technician/ assistant, you should apply to veterinary clinics or hospitals in your area. Prepare a good resumé and submit this to the veterinarian or office manager in each of these clinics. Follow up with a phone call, or request a scheduled visit in which you can speak with the doctor on a personal basis. When meeting with the doctor, be sure that you are dressed neatly and appropriately. Build your self-esteem by giving yourself an ego-boosting lecture first. A display of confidence helps make any interview a winning one!

Good luck!

Joan Workright
3345 Rafel Street
West Pesley, AR 01231
(212)555-1231

August 19, 1996

Donald Jase D.V.M.
JASE Animal Clinic
3345 Donald Street
Jase City, AZ 01231

Dear Dr. Jase,

I have enclosed my resumé for your consideration. During the past twelve years I have accumulated a vast knowledge in a variety of animal-related fields. As you can see, I have worked in two veterinary clinics and kennels, and my specialties have included health, nutrition, and environmental control in both catteries and dog kennels.

I would appreciate an opportunity to meet with yu and discuss how I might best meet the need for assistance at your facility. Perhaps I could see your clinic's operations in order to further determine the specific areas where I could be of greatest value to you. I will call you next week to inquire about an interview.

I am looking forward to meeting you soon,

Sincerely,

Joan Workright

A cover letter enables you to highlight the important things in the resumé

MS. CHELSEA R. CLAYTON

3345 Franklin Avenue • Anytown, USA 55555 • 212 555-7502

Resume

September 21, 1999

The Pawin' Shop
212 Petlover Lane
Anytown, USA 55555
Attention: *Ms. Leah Jameson, Owner*

Position Desired: Sales

1995–Present:
Sales Manager
Cheery-Oh! Pets
Anytown, USA

My responsibilities include customer sales assistance and overseeing employees. Among my other duties, I am in charge of purchasing as well as opening the store on weekends and closing the store Mondays–Wednesdays. I also rotate current stock and set up sales displays, ring up customers, implement methods of reducing loss, and do some light bookkeeping. I am currently seeking new employment as my current employers will soon be retiring from the business.

1992–1995:
Groomer's Assistant
Waggin' Tails Pet Boutique
Anytown, USA

During my time employed at Waggin' Tails Pet Boutique I learned basic grooming and pet care. I am very educated, through my grooming experience, about the many different flea products. As my employers also carried a huge line of feed for retail sale, I have acquired expert knowledge of animal health, nutrition, and diet.

Education:

High School: Anytown Community High School, Anytown, USA
1988–1992

References available upon request.

A resumé should emphasize pet-related skills and experience.

Other
Career
Opportunities

Animal Behavior Consultant

As an animal behavior consultant, you will be expected to solve pet behavior problems. You will need to have a great deal of knowledge of animal behavior to do this! You might consider taking some college-level courses in various aspects of animal behavior. This, of course, is in addition to considerable hands-on experience in working with animals.

You will schedule your clients for one or more (one-hour) session(s) that will result in a behavior modification plan for the pet's owner to follow. You can then make follow-up visits or hold consultations by phone with the client.

In your initial one-hour session, you should go to the client's home and get a full history of the animal and its undesirable behavior. From this information, you can usually determine what is causing the behavior and devise a suitable plan for solving the problem. You may also offer phone consultation service to supplement this treatment. Once you have sufficient credentials, you may work through a veterinarian or groomer referrals.

Newsletter Publishing

If you have a computer and a general knowledge of working with a publishing program, you can design excellent newsletters at home. Your newsletter services may be offered to shelters (to send to their donating members), pet shops (to send to their customers or leave by the check-out as a means of promoting and generating more business), veterinarians (to send as courtesy health update newsletters to their patients), or local pet care news and pet

Being an animal behavior consultant requires a thorough knowledge of animal behavior in general, as well as a complete understanding of each particular pet.

owners' associations. Your newsletter may also soon become valuable as a networking link among these pet-related services and their clients/customers.

Novelty Gift Items

If you are good with crafts and enjoy visiting craft shows, you can design your own animal-related craft line and offer this line at local craft shows, cat shows, or dog shows, or offer your giftware for consignment sales through local gift shops, pet shops and other variety stores.

You might even consider mail-order to pet owners or pet shops, or placing an advertisement for your new line in the various pet publications. Following are some ideas for animal-related crafts:

- Catnip toys
- Fabric-covered pet albums (many beautiful new cat/dog prints are available at your local fabric shop)
- Cat/dog quilts and blankets
- Hand-painted pet portraits or pictures on surfaces such as wood furniture and shelving, canvas, sweat-shirts, purses, cups and any other paintable item
- Wood carvings of different breeds
- Cross-stitch on linens or towels
- Standard quilts, throw pillows or wall hangings made with the new pet-design fabric

A business card is one way of advertising your consulting business.

Novelty items you can design yourself include these:

- Dog or cat trading cards
- Custom-painted mailboxes
- Hand-built and furnished "cat bedrooms" (miniature replicas of the real thing) or "pup" tents

OTHER CAREER OPPORTUNITIES

Dog/Cat Show Concession Booth

....

You will absolutely love this! Traveling is fun, and owning your own "mobile" store is great (lower overhead as compared to traditional stationary pet shops)! This is a terrific way to be your own boss and work only on those days when you feel like it!

Booth space ranges from about $50.00 per show, and you may contact the club sponsoring the show for space rental information. You may need to obtain a state sales license, or more than one if you intend to go to shows in other states. This procedure is usually very simple and one that allows you to purchase certain goods tax-free. The vehicle you will use for transporting your merchandise to and from the shows (usually a van) should be tax-deductible, as are your traveling expenses.

At the show, you will be assigned a booth space, an area of predetermined size and location. You will usually have to provide your own covering as well as your own tables and display equipment at most shows. Some shows may even have specifications on the design and color of your "drape," and local fire ordinances will require the drape you use to be flame-retardant.

Your products can be any variety of items related to either dogs or cats, depending on the type of show. Additionally, you may chose not to carry a variety but to specialize in one product. For example, you may choose to design, make and sell only cat houses. Some suggestions for goods you might carry are dog/cat products (brushes, sweaters, collars) or novelty or handcrafted items such as the ones suggested in this chapter's "Novelty Gift Items."

Visit some local shows and check out the vendors' booths and the items they carry. This will give you a general idea about designing your booth and some specific ideas about products to carry. It is best to avoid competition by concentrating on a product that is not readily available, offering a better variety or better price, or selling unique or hard-to-obtain items.

Commission sales is another idea for selling pet-related products. There are many very talented people who would love the opportunity to display their goods in your booth. Handcrafted items such as these will give your concession booth a personal, "homey" touch and eliminate competition from other vendors who may be carrying generic pet products such as grooming tools or feed dishes.

Supplemental Income Ideas

There are numerous other "mini-career" ideas that are not only novel business ideas but which could benefit an already existing business as an additional means of amplifying your business and supplementing income.

PET-CARE-FOR-KIDS WORKSHOP

Charge an enrollment fee and offer a mini-workshop in pet care training (a brief course that will teach children the basics in pet care) to local children or those in other towns in your state. You can have an established classroom with new classes starting on a weekly or biweekly basis and meeting on certain days each week (depending on the length of your course). Advertise your pet care workshop by posting notices at local veterinary clinics, pet shops, breeders, kennels, groomers, park districts, playgrounds, schools, children's stores, and newspapers.

"LATCHKEY PETS" DAY CARE

Offer day care for puppies, kittens, adult pets, or sick or convalescing pets. You can provide this service in your home or kennel, or in the customer's home. Charges would usually be by the day or week.

One Last Word

Use your imagination! Find a void in the marketplace and "run away" with it. Or *create* a need in the marketplace and establish a means to fill it. Ask yourself, "What is it that I absolutely love to do?" Work this into an imaginative, yet feasible, career plan.

I truly wish you the best of luck!

15

A Brief Guide to Pet Care

Beyond Cats and Dogs

GUINEA PIGS, OR CAVIES

What could be cuter than guinea pigs (more properly called cavies)? I had my first guinea pig when I was very young, and I still delight in the mischievous little "piggys."

Guinea pigs require a "home" that is warm and dry. They enjoy a bedding made of cedar shavings. These shavings should be changed frequently to keep your pet's home dry, clean and sanitary, not to mention smelling nice! Liquid vitamin supplements can be placed in their water supply, and a pellet food that is specifically formulated for guinea pigs should be made available at all times. To prevent tipping or chewing, you should place their feed in a small ceramic crock bowl.

I like to give guinea pigs fresh food daily. This usually includes diced apples, oranges, carrots, spinach or potatoes. I also keep a salt block in with my guinea pigs.

RABBITS

Rabbits should be kept in a caging unit lined with absorbent litter. However, since rabbits are easily "litter-box trained," many owners will allow their pet rabbits to roam freely in the house. If you decide to allow your rabbit the freedom of your home, I recommend that you be aware of potential dangers to the rabbit, such as the pet chewing exposed electrical wires or cords, or damaging your personal items (for example, gnawing on shoes or shredding magazines).

As with guinea pigs, rabbits should receive a liquid vitamin supplement, which may be added to their water bottle. Specially prepared rabbit food in the form of pellets and sun-dried alfalfa (which aids in reducing hairballs) should be left available to your rabbit at all times. Occasionally, you may give your rabbit small amounts of vegetables or fruits, such as apples or carrots.

Your rabbit will enjoy chewing (a favorite pastime, as a matter of fact), and you might find it necessary to provide a chew stick or other chewing material. Caution! Make sure the chewing material you give your pet rabbit has been commercially prepared for such use.

BIRDS

What pretty and amusing creatures they are!

Birds need a source of natural sunlight. When deciding on a location for a bird cage, the ideal choice is the same location as for your houseplants. Avoid "bored birds." Birds do get bored easily, and a bored bird will usually start to pluck out feathers or bombard you with a long screeching serenade. Provide them with plenty of toys or amusing distractions such as metal spoons, mirrors or chains.

Your birds will also enjoy bathing, and you should provide them with a birdbath in their housing unit. Make sure the bath water is *warm* to the touch, *not hot*.

Additionally, a music box placed by a bird's cage will provide many species of birds with peaceful entertainment. Don't forget to talk to your birds, and don't be surprised if they answer back!

Adequate housing is crucial. The cage you select for keeping your bird must be very easy to clean. This means that

Birds make beautiful and amusing pets when properly cared for.

trays, containers and perches must be easily attainable and removable. The cage bars must not be spaced so far apart as to allow your bird to become entrapped between the bars. If you have purchased a new cage, make sure you have washed it thoroughly with hot water and disinfectant to remove any of the manufacturer's gloss. Your bird cage should be of sufficient size to allow a bird free movement without any possibility of injury to wings, tail or feathers. Minimum cage size requirements for most birds are as follows:

- Parakeets, finches, canaries, other small birds: $1 \times 1 \times 2'$
- Cockatiels: $2 \times 2 \times 3'$
- Small Parrots (Conures): $2 \times 3 \times 3'$
- Cockatoos, Amazons, African Greys: $2 \times 3 \times 4'$
- Macaws: $2 \times 4 \times 4'$

Molting

Molting can be stressful on birds. During this period, birds should receive an additional source of protein. You should provide your bird with a quiet place that is warm enough; you may have to raise the room temperature. If your bird breaks a blood feather, locate the feather and pluck it out; the bleeding should stop. The entire molting process will take about six weeks.

Feather Plucking and Other Signs of Illness or Stress

A bird that plucks at feathers might be bored or stressed. Two common sources of stress are another bird, or a cage that is too small or confining. More likely though, excessive feather plucking is caused by parasites such as mites or lice. Find the surce of your bird's plucking, and correct it as quickly as possible. Plucking is a definite sign of trouble in birds. Fluffed-out feathers may be a sign that your bird is chilled. If your bird's feathers appear to be ruffled and this is accompanied by a nasal discharge, darkened nasal feathers, or a lethargic appearance, your bird may be suffering from a respiratory problem. *This requires immediate veterinary attention.*

If you suspect your bird may be sick, always consult your veterinarian immediately. Health problems in birds tend to progress very rapidly, and death can occur in a matter of a few days.

Notes on Kittens and Puppies

Between the ages of six weeks and four months, your kitten or puppy should be receiving a high-quality kitten or puppy food, four times a day. Between the ages of four months and eight months, they need three meals a day. Kittens as well as puppies over eight months require one to two meals per day.

Feed a well-balanced food that is specifically made for the kind of animal you have, as cats and dogs each have very complex dietary requirements that are unique to their species. It is due to these unique nutritional needs that cats and dogs each require special diets that have been scientifically formulated for that species' proper nutritional balance.

Puppies require special attention and dietary considerations.

Additionally, I recommend adding vitamin/mineral supplements to *one* of your pet's meals each day. And make sure your pet has fresh water available at all times.

Begin grooming at an early age so your pet will become accustomed to the grooming procedure. Your short-haired cat or dog should receive a daily or weekly brushing with a soft-bristled brush. This ensures healthier skin, cleaner fur, and less shedding on your furniture. Your long-haired cat or dog will require daily or semiweekly combing or brushing in order to maintain a tangle-free coat (and, in cats, to reduce the additional risk of hairballs).

Early dental care is also recommended. Remember to never put your fingers behind your dog or cat's teeth. This can result in the most painful bite imaginable!

Provide your kitty with a clean litter box that is in a convenient location (for kitty, that is). If you find your kitty is not using the litter pan, try changing the brand of kitty litter you use. This may help, as some chemicals in certain litters can be irritating to cats' paw pads, making them avoid the litter box altogether. I have known of cats that would only use their litter tray if shredded paper was used in place of commercial litter.

Never put a collar on your cat, unless it is the breakaway kind! A cat that is allowed to run free can get caught on a branch or other object and choke, starve or dehydrate before being located or rescued. If you allow a cat to run free, however, not only is there the danger of death by an automobile, but it will be nearly impossible for anyone to return a lost cat without a collar and tag. If you place a collar on your cat, cut it three-fourths of an inch through so that it will break easily if kitty does get caught on something. Other precautions to take are keeping the doors of washing machines and dryers closed (your kitty may climb inside unbeknownst to you).

Always put a collar and tag on your dog!

Many of the aforementioned hazards are also dangerous to dogs. Rocking chairs and windows and deck railing in upper-floor rooms or apartments are dangers to dogs as well. I also have heard of cats and dogs burning their paws on stoves with electric burners (because electric burners do not cool down as quickly as do gas stove burners). Swimming pools also pose a hazard to inquisitive animals, as they can fall into them and are then unable to climb out. Contrary to popular belief, not all dogs can swim.

Try to pet-proof your home. Look at your home through the eyes of your pets. What possible hazards do you see? If you find any, work at eliminating them.

SPAYING AND NEUTERING

An alarming 25 million homeless pets are born each year in the United States alone. Of these, approximately 15 million will be destroyed or used for research. The unfortunate 10 million that remain will usually face starvation or death from disease. It costs us an unbelievably staggering price tag of $500 million each year to capture, shelter and kill these unwanted pets! These are 25 million reasons to convince you that you should spay or neuter your pet.

Neutering a male cat will (almost always) eliminate the problem of a spraying tom, if done before the habit of spraying is established. Neutering a male dog before five months of age greatly reduces aggressiveness toward other dogs and diminishes the instinct to fight. Neutering does *not* make a dog gain weight. Overfeeding, combined with inactivity, causes obesity in dogs and cats. Fat, lazy animals are the owner's fault and are not due to spaying or neutering.

There are many other advantages of spaying and neutering. The health benefits alone are just some of the very evident and justifiable reasons for spaying or neutering your pet. A spayed female will live an average of two years longer than an unspayed female. Her risk of developing acute metritis (inflammation of the uterus), endometritis (inflammation of the lining of the uterus) and pyometra (uterine abscess) is eliminated; and her risk of developing mammary tumors or breast cancer is practically none. I haven't even mentioned the risk to her health (and life) she avoids by not having to go through labor and delivery!

In males, neutering eliminates the risk of testicular tumors and prostate gland enlargement.

All in all, what better reasons (beyond the 530 million reasons just mentioned) could you have to justify not spaying or neutering your pet? NONE!

16

Marketing for Success— Don't Let Your Business Fail!

Nearly 90 percent of all business failures are due to lack of marketing, or poor marketing skills and advertising management. It is important that you learn all you can about marketing your service. It is equally important that you learn the proper way to manage an advertising campaign. An alarming half of all retail advertising is wasted! Careful structure of a promotional marketing plan will greatly reduce costly advertising mistakes.

When you devise a marketing plan, you are not just outlining a way to sell your product or service. You are discovering what your service is doing, and why—also, in effect, what will be accomplished by doing it. You need to understand your advertising goals and objectives, and develop a suitable marketing campaign for reaching these goals within an established time frame.

First and foremost, you should determine an appropriate advertising budget, perhaps a 5 percent allowance of your operating capital. Next, choose your advertising media. Once you have done that, design your strategy around this. Be creative and imaginative, or invest in an advertising agency that specializes in your type of business. Sometimes these agencies can receive good prices or special deals on television or radio commercial spots. From there, devise a suitable plan for marketing your particular product or service.

Marketing Time and Money

How much time and money you have available plays a key role in the marketing method you will chose. Let's take a look at some marketing methods that may be beneficial to you:

Publicity from Press Releases Press releases should never describe your services, or its values. Instead, a good press release will be an informative article that *suggests* what your business' services are. For example, your press release should *not* state, "PomPom Palace offers professional grooming for all breeds. We have been in business for 20 years and have the experience to groom your pet to the exact Standard of the breed." Among other reasons, this is *not* effective advertising because editors will not think the fact that you offer professional grooming as being all that noteworthy. Nor is the fact that you have been in business for twenty years the "news flash" of the week! A good press release states something that the *reader* will be *interest*ed in and, at the same time, gets your business' point across. A better press release could read something like this:

SUMMER HINTS FOR PET OWNERS

"Summer can be hard on your pet," says Paula Pom, who has operated PomPom Palace of Yourtown since 1973. "Animals can really suffer from the heat." Paula gives a few pointers on caring for your pet this summer:

- Keep your pet free of summer pests. Make it a daily habit to check your pet for fleas and ticks.

- You should also ask your vet about heartworm prevention. Heartworm is the result of a bite by a mosquito carrying the deadly heartworm parasite *Dirofilaria immitis*. This parasite then enters the bloodstream, where it travels to the heart. In the heart, the larvae mature to adulthood. If left untreated, heartworm can kill a pet by damaging the heart, lungs, liver and kidneys.

- NEVER leave your pet in a closed car. The temperature in a closed car can reach dangerously high levels in a very few minutes, causing DEATH.

- Make sure you provide your pet with an easily accessible area of cool shade in which to hide from summer's heat.

- Always have plenty of fresh water available.

This summer, Paula is offering a free pamphlet on summer pet care. To get your free copy, call PomPom Palace at (012) 345-6789.

Notice how this press release has established recognition for Paula's grooming shop. In addition, Paula has impressed upon the public that she is an experienced and knowledgeable groomer who has a great deal of genuine compassion for pets. Another bonus to this press release is that it will enable Paula, through the phone calls people make to her store, to acquire a mailing list for direct mail to new customers.

Direct Mail Direct mail can be focused on a special, targeted list of individual consumers; commercial inserts in local publications; or in response to direct inquiries.

Classified and Display Ads Put them in trade publications, newspapers, billboards and signs.

Trade Shows, County Fair Exhibits, Pet Shows and Other Consumer Shows You can rent an exhibitor's space or a display booth

Person-to-Person Selling and Telemarketing This involves sales calls, by phone or in person, to prospective customers, usually those who have shown an interest in

"Summer can be hard on your pet, so it's important to take extra precautions." Special tips like these show customers you're a good source of information and care deeply for their animals.

your kind of services. One way to generate leads is to offer free information. For example, if your service is pet referral, you might offer a free informative pamphlet on selecting the proper pet for your family and lifestyle, with additional pointers on pet care. You could place this offer in an advertisement asking the customer to send a SASE to your business address. You may wish to include a coupon worth a small discount on your service. And remember to print your business name on your pamphlet!

Free Estimates and Donation of Your Services You provide these to local projects and causes. Participate in community events where your name will be recognized and mentioned as a contributor.

Yellow Page Listing Customers often make their decisions strictly by looking through the yellow page ads in their local telephone book. (Yes, sometimes bigger is better.)

Radio and Television Buying small spots on local cable or radio channels may not be costly, usually reaches a larger audience, and can yield higher returns than many other forms of advertising.

Promotional Advertising Giveaways Promotional advertising items are a good, economical way to "pass your name around." Some ideas are calendars, magnets, letter openers, lighters, keyrings, balloons, buttons, ice scrapers, pens, brochures and flyers, Christmas cards, bulletins and, yes, even doggie "pickup" bags!

Word-of-Mouth Word-of-mouth is probably the single best way to build your business. It includes networking and referrals from other people. A common misunderstanding about service-oriented businesses is the notion that if you deliver good service the referrals will happen automatically. Usually this is *not* the case. Even if you consistently provide excellent service, you still may not get enough referrals to sustain you, unless the services you provide are in very high demand.

Never underestimate the power of word-of-mouth advertising, and never take referrals for granted. Once you start getting referrals and your business becomes self-sustaining, don't ever assume that it will stay that way. Many things can happen: The market can change, resulting in your service becoming less in demand . . . the economy can change (as it inevitably does), making your service unapproachable, or too costly.

To stimulate word-of-mouth referrals, it is essential that you pass along a business card to every person you meet. You must take advantage of every opportunity to generate as many referrals as possible. Chances are that if you tell two friends, then they will tell two friends, and well, you know the rest . . . .

Public Relations/Recognition—Literature, Logos and Apearance   Create newsletters containing personal, product or service communications. Provide direct customer service through sales force or sales leads. Design the product or service's name and physical appearance, packaging and labeling. Sell the product, company or service's value to the customer. Make company brochures, catalogs/price lists. Use company vehicles and employee or staff uniforms. Print up company stationery and/or business cards.

Nothing will sell a customer faster than *your success*. After all, if you are successful, there must be a reason! It is important that you create a successful, professional image of yourself and your company. You should have attractively designed business cards, stationery and other correspondence material. Your service vehicles should be clean and pleasing to the eye. Your company's name should be professionally imprinted, and prominently displayed, on all company vehicles. Your company's telephone should be answered by a person who has been properly trained in phone etiquette. After all, this telephone conversation may often be the first impression a customer gains of you!

Creating a Good Business Image

Your business' position in the pet industry is not something you do to your company, but rather something you do to your clients (this means the particular way you want to have your clients perceive you)! Your image in the marketplace is the backbone of your business. To find out what your company's professional image, or "position," is in the market, you must first analyze your company's strengths and goals:

- Where does the need for your service fit into today's marketplace?

- What value does your service have, and why should potential customers commit to you?

- How do you want your customer to see you: friendly, fun, serious, honest, hardworking? How does this differ from your competitors' positions in the community?

- How will your image/position stand out over your competitors'? You must build an image that will make your customer select you over your competitors.

You must position yourself for success! For example, a local woodworker, who specialized in quality handcrafted front doors, found business starting to slack off. The woodworker thought about his professional image and concluded that, in order to gain new business, he needed an improved image in the community's mind. After much thought, he decided to specialize in the distinct "personalization" of each wood door. The woodworker then began to offer an elegant engraving of the customer's name right on the front of the door! The doors were so attractive and unusual that even customers who didn't need new doors were soon seeking the woodworker's services. This craftsman's market image/position was enhanced by his being perceived as the only woodworker in town who offered this unique customizing service. By gaining this special and unique identity, he soon stood out from competitors and became a success. What's in a name? Everything! If you want to inspire your customers to do business with you, give yourself a designer label! Would you rather eat at "Fanny's Fish Stop" or "Morgan's by the Sea"?

What about your motto? Your professional statement is just as important as your name. It should be a statement that identifies you in the way you would like your customers to perceive you. For instance, your motto could be reliable and solid, such as "Dog's Best Friend." Many companies will use slogans as well. Your slogan may be something catchy, such as "Give us a call . . . we'll treat you like a dog (and that's very good)!" A deck company might have the slogan "Give us a call . . .we'd love to deck you!"; a casual-wear clothing shop, "Come on in and let us 'un-dress' you!" By giving yourself a motto or slogan, you are projecting an image that will position your company as one which provides a particular type of quality service.

Advertising—Do It Like the Pros

Professional advertising agencies approach advertising and marketing in a very organized, methodical way. They develop what is known as a "plan of attack" and then they follow through on this plan. Unfortunately, we can't all afford the professional services of an advertising agency.

However, we can devise our own method of "attack" and follow it through. You should plan your campaign strategy utilizing the marketing methods I have laid out for you here. You can save money by designing your own ads using any PC, Macintosh or other computer system and a good publishing software program.

Design is important to your ad. You do not want your ad to be cluttered, with many different typefaces and only a small eye-catching area. Your ad should have a good deal of "white space" surrounding it so that the customers focus on your statement. With a cluttered ad, the customer will get lost in all the gibberish. Your headline should contain an attention-getting statement that might contain one of these persuasive, eye-catching words: "Save," "Free," "Guarantee," "Easy," "You" or "Proven."

Repetitious ad placement, however, is still the single most important aspect of advertising. The average person will look at your advertisement three times before actually

Fish Sale

Buy one—get second one for half-price!

Angels ◆ Mollies ◆ Barbs

Platys ◆ Gouramis

and more...

This Saturday and Sunday only!

The Fisherfolk Shop
555 Main Street ◆ Yourtown

Your ad should be eye-catching and uncluttered.

seeing it! Most ads need to be seen seven times before people actually consider a company valid. This means that you must place an ad 21 times before it becomes effective! Do you see the importance of repetition? Small business owners must not make the mistake of changing the ad (or its style) because they haven't received a response the first few times it appeared. Rarely, if ever, will a person get an immediate response to ads. It is much wiser to place the same small ad repeatedly in the same general area, over several weeks, than to place a costly display ad once in a while. When it comes to small space ads, or display ads, bigger is not always better! Being *recognized through repetition is the single most important factor!*

Customizing—Making a Marketing Plan That Works for You

Following are eight questions whose answers can lead to a successful marketing plan. These steps are described and explained in more detail elsewhere in this chapter. Please read the entire section on marketing before devising your own marketing plan. Answers to these questions along with those in the following section will help you devise a plan unique to your needs:

1. How much time and money do you have to invest in your marketing campaign?
2. What will be your marketing methods?

3. What will you name your company? What will be your slogan or motto? How will you create a business image that sells itself, and what image will that be?

4. How will you reach your targeted audience? Have you found or established a "niche"?

5. How will you network your business? Will you use word-of-mouth or other business referrals?

6. How will you establish a good advertising campaign? Devise display ads that sell.

7. How will you create the impression of being successful, even if you are just starting out?

8. What methods will you use to scout for new business?

Business Self-Analysis—The Essentials for Completing a Successful Marketing Outline

A. *Describe your business* in 50 words or less. Example: I am a contracting service that specializes in custom-built kennels.

B. *How does your service benefit others?* Example: Customers benefit from my service because I provide quality-built kennels; guarantees on workmanship and materials; and expert advice and planning concerning weatherproofing and climate control, customer convenience, and animal safety measures and precautions. By specializing in custom-built kennels for the past 20 years, I have saved my customers time and expense through my vast experience and knowledge. The customers are satisfied with my work and reliability.

C. *Who is your competition?* Example: My competition consists solely of a multiservice contracting company. I plan to meet my competition head-on by promoting a fact-based advertising plan stating my specialization in custom-built kennels, with over 1,000 satisfied customers. I plan to use "validation" in my advertising to give it more credibility, by utilizing actual customers' testimonials. I plan a strategy of competing based on an expertly devised advertising campaign. My marketing concept consists of advertisements that focus on stating (to my potential customers) the benefits they will receive by using my service. (People want to know how they will benefit from a service.)

D. *How do you want to be perceived* by your customers? What are your positioning or (core) image-making statements? Example: I would like to be perceived as a reliable company that genuinely cares about the customers' needs. I would like to be recognized for being an honest, friendly, reliable, and knowledgeable service provider with emphasis on giving the customer top-quality work and products.

E. *Describe your target audience.* Example: My targeted market includes private and boarding kennels, veterinarians, pet care facilities, and general pet owners alike.

F. *How will you market your service?* Example: Obtain mailing lists of my targeted market. I will send out an attractive and informative brochure promoting my service to approximately 100 targeted consumers each month. I also intend to capture the general pet-owning public and gain a recognizable name through repetition in advertising; placing the same ad on a regular basis in area newspapers and pet-specific publications. Additionally, I will post flyers in strategic spots that have a high degree of visibility to my targeted market, such as pet shops, veterinary clinics, boarding kennels and grooming shops.

G. *What methods will you use to advertise?* Where will you use these methods? Example: Place ads on a regular basis in local newspapers. I plan on having my ads remain consistent to gain trust and recognition through repetition. I will utilize referrals and network through word-of-mouth. I intend to gain reputable testimonials to publish, in order to gain more customer trust and credibility. I plan on getting my name out and recognized through trade shows, fair exhibits, and other community gatherings. I will strategically place flyers and business cards, and do a direct mailing to appropriate consumers (my targeted market). I plan on submitting press releases which reflect upon the reliability of my company.

H. *What are your service policies?* Will you grant credit terms, extended payment plans or customer discounts? What about guarantees, charges on materials and labor, and returns? Example: My services will be offered mainly on a prepaid basis. I will consider half-down, and a partial payment plan on the balance, to qualified customers. Any customer with a justifiable cause who wishes a refund will gain an appropriate prorated return, or an entire refund, as the case requires.

I. Is *your pricing in line with industry norms?* That is to say: Does your present market economy warrant your pricing? What about your competition? How does your pricing compare with theirs? Would lowering or raising your prices affect your returns? If prices are reduced, is your decreased pricing significant enough to make a profit? Will your customers question the quality of your goods or services because of these low prices? If you increase your prices, can you justify this by offering your customers a better product or service, over that of your competitors?

Do you offer something special or unique? In other words, do you realistically believe that your clients are willing to pay a higher price for your service (over your competitor's lower PRICES) because of the special benefits that you, and you alone, offer them?

Planning is the first step on the road to business success. Planning is based on knowing your business, your market, your competition, your resources and yourself. Once you are armed with that knowledge, you're already on the road to success. Good luck!

Index

A

AdSOS, 36–37
Advertising. *See also* Marketing
  of all-breed pet care services,
    92
  of animal photography, 120
  design of ad in, 217
  of exotic pet shops, 50
  of grooming-station leasing,
    77–78
  of grooming-station rentals, 75
  of kennel services, 22
  of mail-order sypply businesses,
    129–31
  of pet referral services, 149–51
  of pet-sitting services, 109
  of pet supply shops, 30
  professional approach to,
    217–19
Advertising agencies, 209, 217
Air flow, in kennels, 10
Airport services, 83–84
All-breed pet care services,
    81–94
  airport pickup and delivery,
    83–84
  animal training, 86
  career school programs for, 163
  customer relations in, 92
  exercising and walking, 85
  feeding, nutritional planning
    and medicating, 83
  grooming and coat care, 82
  kennel/cattery assistance, 86
  kennel cleaning, 83
  lost-pet recovery, 88–89
  operations of, 93–94
  pet paramedic, 92
  pet placement, 87

  pet referral, 89–91
  temporary employee
    placement, 91
  veterinary referral,
    87–88
  veterinary taxi, 84
Amphibians, 46
Animal behavior consultants, 187
Animal clubs/associations, 89,
    120, 147, 170
Animal photography,
    117–23
  equipment for, 119–20
  settings for, 117–19
  specifics of, 122–23
Animal training, 86
Annual membership fees, 151
Aquarium maintenance/
    leasing, 43, 97–104
  billing for, 104
  contracts for, 103
  employees in, 99–100
  equipment for, 101–3
Attorney consultation, 77, 94,
    103, 139
Aviary owner/operator programs,
    161–62

B

Bathing, instructions for, 59
Bathrooms, for kennels, 6
Billing, 103–4
Birds, 198–201
Black scorpions, 47
Bookkeeping. *See* Recordkeeping
Breeder referral services. *See* Pet
    referral services
Breed listing sheets, 145–46, 148
Breed Standard, 172
Brochures

INDEX